Understanding Pensions

With birth rates falling at the same time that average age is rising in the developed world, the pensions time bomb is ticking more loudly than ever. Understanding how pensions work, their history and their future is absolutely essential.

This book thoroughly explains to readers the unique concepts and terminology which underpin pensions. It focuses first on the rationale for pensions and their evolution, before moving on to an explanation of the latest controversies regarding pensions. The glossary of pensions terminology in the final section of the book virtually ensures its place on many academic bookshelves.

This timely volume is an extremely useful contribution to this important issue. Of use to policy-makers as much as to students and academics of finance and public policy, *Understanding Pensions* should prove to be a popular addition to the literature.

Martin Sullivan is a Senior Lecturer in Economics, University of the West of England, Bristol, UK.

Routledge international studies in money and banking

Understanding Pensions

Martin Sullivan

LONDON AND NEW YORK

First published 2004
by Routledge
2 Park Square, Milton Park, Abingdon, Oxon, OX14 4RN

Simultaneously published in the USA and Canada
by Routledge
270 Madison Avenue, New York, NY 10016

Routledge is an imprint of the Taylor & Francis Group

© 2004 Martin Sullivan

Typeset in Times by Wearset Ltd, Boldon, Tyne and Wear
Printed and bound in Great Britain by MPG Books Ltd, Bodmin

British Library Cataloguing in Publication Data
A catalogue record for this book is available from the British Library

Library of Congress Cataloging in Publication Data
A catalog record for this book has been requested

ISBN 0-415-27389-7

For Kerstin

Contents

PART 3
An A–Z of Pensions 111

Figures

Tables

Acknowledgements

This book could not have been written without the help and support of numerous friends and colleagues. Thanks are especially due, however, to Kerstin, for her unswerving encouragement; Dru Esam, for her invaluable assistance with every aspect of the book's preparation; Peter Howells, for his helpful comments on the draft; and David Allen, whose spreadsheet skills are legendary and without whose help the graphical illustrations in the book would be much poorer. Any errors or defects the book might contain are, of course, the author's sole responsibility.

Abbreviations

ABI	Association of British Insurers
ABO	Accrued Benefit Obligation
ACA	Association of Consulting Actuaries
ACT	Advance Corporation Tax
AFPs	Asociaciones de Fondos de Pensiones
APP	Approved Personal Pension
ASB	Accounting Standards Board
AVCs	Additional Voluntary Contributions
BIM	Bishopsgate Investment Management
BSP	Basic State Pension
CARE	Career Average Revalued Earnings
CPF	Central Provident Fund
DB	Defined Benefit
DC	Defined Contribution
DRC	Delayed Retirement Credit
DSS	Department of Social Security
DTC	Dividend Tax Credit
DWP	Department for Work and Pensions
ERISA	Employee Retirement Income Security Act
EU	European Union
FASB	Financial Accounting Standards Board
FRS 17	Financial Reporting Standard 17
FSA	Financial Services Authority
FSAVCs	Free-Standing Additional Voluntary Contributions
GAD	Government Actuary's Department
GAR	Guaranteed Annuity Rate
GDP	Gross Domestic Product
GMC	Guaranteed Minimum Contribution
GMP	Guaranteed Minimum Pension
GPPP	Group Personal Pension Plan
GPS	Graduated Pension Scheme
HRP	Home Responsibilities Protection
IBO	Indexed Benefit Obligation

IRAs	Individual Retirement Accounts
LAUTRO	Life Assurance and Unit Trust Regulatory Organisation
LEL	Lower Earnings Limit
LPI	Limited Price Indexation
MCC	Maxwell Communications Corporation
MFR	Minimum Funding Requirement
MGN	Mirror Group Newspapers
MIG	Minimum Income Guarantee
MNT	Member Nominated Trustee
MWR	Married Women's Rate
NAPF	National Association of Pension Funds
NDC	Notional Defined Contribution
NI	National Insurance
NICs	National Insurance Contributions
OASDI	Old-Age, Survivors and Disability Insurance
OECD	Organisation for Economic Cooperation and Development
OMO	Open Market Option
OPB	Occupational Pensions Board
OPRA	Occupational Pensions Regulatory Authority
PAYG	Pay-As-You-Go
PBGC	Pension Benefit Guarantee Corporation
PBO	Projected Benefit Obligation
PCB	Pensions Compensation Board
PPF	Pension Protection Fund
PPP	Personal Pension Plan
PRF	Personal Retirement Fund
RPI	Retail Prices Index
S2P	State Second Pension
SAS	Self-Administered Scheme
SERPS	State Earnings-Related Pension Scheme
SFO	Serious Fraud Office
SGC	Superannuation Guarantee Charge
SIB	Securities and Investments Board
SIP	Statement of Investment Principles
SIPP	Self Invested Personal Pension
SMPI	Statutory Money Purchase Illustration
SPA	State Pension Age
SSAP	Statement of Standard Accounting Practice
SSAS	Small Self-Administered Scheme
SSB	Short Service Benefit
UEL	Upper Earnings Limit
UFPS	Unified Funded Pension Scheme

Introduction

Benjamin Franklin once famously remarked that there were two certainties in life, death and taxes. When Franklin made this observation, in the eighteenth century, most people died young. We should not be surprised, then, that he did not include living to a ripe old age in his list of life's certainties. Living to a great age is not a certainty today. For growing numbers of people, though, it is a distinct possibility. Children born in the year 2000 in France, Germany, the UK and the USA can, on average, expect to live for more than 77 years. Their Japanese counterparts have an average life expectancy of over 80 years. In Britain, the number of congratulatory messages the Queen sends each year to new centenarians has quadrupled since she was crowned in 1953. What is more, life expectancy is projected to go on rising in the coming decades.

Unlike longevity, the length of time people typically spend in paid employment has not been increasing. In fact, the opposite has happened. Since the 1970s, the average age at which people in Britain and many other developed countries cease working for a living has been falling steadily. In other words, there has been a significant increase in the proportion of peoples' lives spent in retirement. This has raised pensions to a level of importance never seen before. In the past, pensions were a means by which people insured against the unlikely event that they would become too old to support themselves by working. Today, pensions act more like retirement endowments, because most people can expect to stop working long before they die.

Pensions have long been the subject of fierce controversy. Although few would argue against the need for pensions, a debate has raged for more than a century over the most appropriate way to provide them. This is because pensions can be provided through a variety of mechanisms which differ in their advantages and disadvantages. The debate is not just about the pros and cons of one approach to pension provision compared with another, but about whether, and how, different approaches can be combined to produce an optimal retirement income system. Although the intensity of the debate has ebbed and flowed over time, it has never been stronger than it is at present.

It is not the purpose of this book to enter directly into the current debate about pensions. Rather, it aims to shed light on the issues being debated by providing a clear and accessible guide to the unique language and concepts of pensions. It is intended to be a source of information and analysis which will be of interest to academics, students, pension industry practitioners, journalists and those with a general interest in the subject of pensions. Information is presented on the pension arrangements in various countries, including Australia, Britain, Germany, Italy and the United States. The constraints of time and space, however, make a comprehensive analysis of different national pension systems impracticable. The British pension system is described and analysed in the greatest depth. There are two reasons for this. First, Britain is the country whose pension arrangements the author knows most about. Second, lessons can be learned from Britain's recent pensions experience which have relevance for other countries.

The book is organised into three distinct parts. Part 1, Pensions: Principles and Practice, considers the rationale for pension provision, describes the evolution of public and private pensions and explores the ways in which pensioners' incomes have changed over time. It also outlines the perceived demographic challenges to public pension schemes and considers different national responses to these challenges. Part 2, Pensions: Issues and Controversies, provides analysis of a range of contemporary issues in the areas of public and private pension provision. Uncertainty is a major theme in the analysis of these issues. Section 2.1, for example, highlights the speculative nature of population projections and casts doubt on the argument that public pension schemes will ultimately be blown apart by a 'demographic time bomb'. Other important themes running through the analysis in Part 2 are paternalism, choice, fairness and the role of regulation. Finally, Part 3 consists of an extensive glossary of pensions and related terminology.

Part 1

Pensions

Principles and practice

1.1 PENSIONS AND PENSION SCHEMES

In all developed countries, retired people represent a substantial share of the total population (Figure 1.1.1). For the vast majority of these people, pension payments constitute the bulk of their retirement incomes. A pension is an income received by a retired person in place of earnings from employment. Pensions are not the only source of income available to retired people. Other sources include income from property, savings and investments, means-tested state benefits and, sometimes, the right to consume free of charge – or at a discount – goods or services which non-pensioners must pay for. Many pensioners also have access to a share of the incomes of other people with whom they live, and many continue to perform some paid work (Figure 1.1.2). The difference between a pension and other forms of income is that pensions take the form of an annuity – a stream of regular payments, guaranteed for life.

The need for pensions arises because people's capacity to work, and consequently their ability to derive an income from employment, declines in later life. Although the point at which this decline begins, and the rate at which it occurs, differs between individuals, everyone's capacity to support themselves from employment eventually ceases altogether, unless death intervenes first. In traditional societies and less economically developed countries, families provide the bulk of economic support for the elderly. More than half of all old people in the world are cared for by their relatives. The extended family structures found in traditional societies and developing countries are, however, much less common in the industrialised world. Economic linkages between family members are weaker.

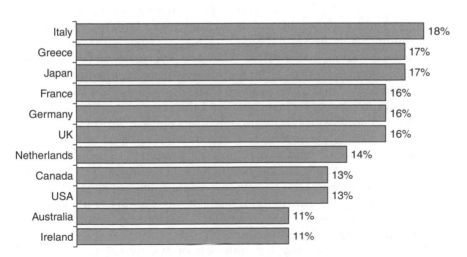

Figure 1.1.1 People aged 65 and over as a proportion of the total population in selected countries, 2000 (US Census Bureau International Database).

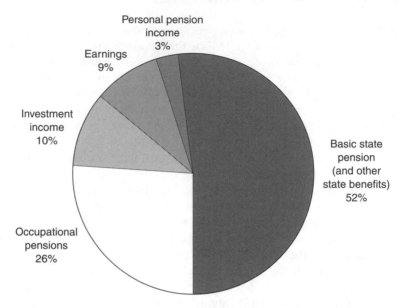

Figure 1.1.2 Estimated percentage shares of UK pensioner units' gross incomes by source, 2001–2002 (DWP (2003)).

Kinship groups are smaller and more widely dispersed, and relatively few households comprise more than two generations of the same family. Pensions are thus a necessary substitute in developed countries for economic support within the family.

A pension scheme is a mechanism for providing retired people with annuities, and for allowing those of working age to build up entitlements to an annuity when they retire. Pension schemes can be provided publicly, by national governments, or privately, by employers, insurance companies and other commercial organisations. Without pension schemes, the only way workers could make provision for their old age would be by deferring consumption of part of their income until they retired – i.e. by saving for retirement. Faced with uncertain life expectancies, however, workers would have difficulty knowing how much to save. Those with a strong aversion to risk would tend to over-save, in an attempt to avoid the possibility of exhausting their savings before they died. Others would not save enough. Pension schemes overcome these pitfalls by providing retirement annuities in return for contributions made during working years. They are, therefore, a more efficient way of shifting consumption from the early to the latter part of the human life course.

Pension schemes usually fall into one of two broad types: defined benefit (DB) schemes and defined contribution (DC) schemes. DB schemes allow workers to accrue entitlements to retirement benefits, the value of which are determined by the rules of the scheme. DB schemes provide either flat-rate or earnings-related benefits. Britain's basic state pension (BSP) is an example of a flat-rate DB scheme. In April 2003, single pensioners with full BSP entitlement received pension payments of £77.45 per week, irrespective of their prior earnings from employment. Married or cohabiting pensioner couples received £123.80 per week. The US equivalent of Britain's BSP – known as Old Age Survivors and Disability Insurance (OASDI) – is an earnings-related scheme. The value of the pension benefits it provides depends upon pensioners' earnings before retirement. Pension entitlements are calculated as a fraction of workers' pre-retirement earnings for each year of scheme participation. Thus, the greater a person's earnings from employment, the higher the pension benefits he or she will receive in retirement.

Whereas the value of pension payments from DB schemes is predetermined according to benefit rules, contributions are variable. The administrators of DB schemes are free to raise or lower contribution levels in line with their scheme's financing requirements. DB schemes can thus be thought of as providing fixed benefits based upon variable contributions. By contrast, DC schemes provide variable pensions based on fixed contributions. The rules of DC schemes specify the amounts that must be contributed, not how much will be paid out in pension benefits. Contributions may be flat-rate – e.g. £50 per month – or set at a fixed proportion of workers' earnings. DC schemes are frequently referred to as money purchase schemes, since the value of the pensions they provide depends upon how much pension income a worker's total contributions will buy when he or she retires.

Pension schemes are financed on either a funded or a pay-as-you-go (PAYG) basis. Contributions to funded schemes accumulate in a fund which is invested in a range of financial assets – company shares, government and commercial bonds, property, etc. The pensions these schemes provide are paid for from members' accumulated contributions and investment returns. Contributions to PAYG schemes do not accumulate in a fund. Instead, the pensions these schemes provide are financed directly from contributions. Because there is no fund, PAYG schemes are often referred to as unfunded schemes. Whereas DB schemes can be financed on either a funded or PAYG basis, DC schemes are always funded.

A key distinction between funding and PAYG is that those who contribute to funded schemes pay for their own pensions, whereas contributors to PAYG schemes pay someone else's pension. Because PAYG schemes finance retirement benefits from the contributions of active members – those currently in employment – they can begin paying pensions as soon as they are established. A disadvantage of funded schemes is that many years must elapse from the time they are set up before sufficient funds have accumulated to provide retiring workers with pension benefits.

Differences in national pension systems are often compared and analysed with reference to various 'pillars', or 'tiers', of pension provision. Although three pillars/tiers are typically identified, opinions differ over how these should be defined (Turner 1998). A straightforward approach is to define each of the pillars/tiers according to the different providers of pensions. Thus, the first pillar – the bottom tier – comprises state-run public pension schemes, the second pillar – the middle tier – is made up of employer-provided occupational pensions, and the third pillar – the top tier – consists of pension arrangements which individuals make for themselves through commercial pension providers. Alternatively, each pillar/tier can be defined in terms of different types of pension benefit. In this case, the first pillar would provide flat-rate pensions, the second earnings-related pensions, with the third providing pension benefits which vary according to the amount of retirement saving individuals undertake.

The different pillars/tiers of pension provision can also be defined in terms of their function or their method of financing. On a functional basis, the first pillar is defined as consisting of basic income schemes aimed at preventing poverty in old age through the provision of flat-rate retirement benefits. The second pillar is made up of income maintenance schemes, which aim to prevent a sudden fall in income at retirement by providing earnings-related benefits. The third pillar consists of schemes designed to supplement the retirement incomes provided by the first and second pillars. Where the different pillars/tiers are defined according to the method of financing, the first pillar consists of schemes which are financed out of general taxation. These usually provide means-tested retirement benefits. Pillars two and three comprise, respectively, PAYG-financed government schemes and funded private occupational and individual schemes.

Membership of more than one pension scheme is common in Britain, the United States and many other countries. In addition to their participation in the government-run scheme, British and American workers are frequently members of schemes provided by their employers. Many workers also contribute to schemes run by commercial pension providers, either in addition to or in place of those offered by their employers. Consequently, large numbers of people either have, or will have, a total pension income that derives from several sources. In some countries, though – Greece and Italy, for example – membership of more than one pension scheme is unusual. The overwhelming majority of workers in these countries rely solely on the government scheme for their retirement pensions.

Participation in pension schemes is not always a matter of choice. Where governments provide a public scheme, membership is usually compulsory. Although participation in private schemes is often voluntary, as in the UK and US, in some countries – Australia and Chile, for example – it is compulsory. Even in countries where people have the right but not the obligation to join a private scheme, governments frequently offer financial incentives for them to do so. Typical incentives are tax relief on contributions to private schemes and the right to opt out of part or all of the public scheme. In Britain, where there are two public schemes (the BSP and a Second State Pension, (S2P), exemption from participation in S2P is granted to individuals who have joined a qualifying private scheme.

Contributing to a pension scheme is not risk free. Members of pension schemes face two kinds of risk. First, there is the risk that the amount of retirement income they ultimately receive will be substantially less than they had hoped for or expected. Second, there is the possibility that achieving their desired level of retirement income will turn out to be more costly than was originally anticipated. These risks arise because of the long-term and illiquid nature of pension saving. Because pension contributions are made over several decades, there is plenty of time for a scheme's actual performance to deviate from what was originally promised or expected. Moreover, if contributors become dissatisfied with the performance of their schemes, moving their pension savings to another scheme may be impossible or extremely expensive.

1.2 PUBLIC PENSIONS

Public pension schemes – also known as state pension schemes – are organised by national governments. They aim either to prevent poverty in old age, through the provision of flat-rate retirement benefits, or to ensure that workers' incomes are maintained after retirement by linking the value of pension payments to earnings from employment. Pensions are usually payable in return for contributions made over several decades by employees and their employers. The vast majority of public schemes are run on a PAYG basis, where the cost of providing retired workers with pensions is met from the contributions of those currently in employment. Thus, public schemes work by redistributing income directly from workers to pensioners. Those in employment are willing to pay their predecessors' pensions on the understanding that the next generation of workers will do the same for them.

Germany was the first country to introduce a public pension scheme, in 1889, followed by, amongst others, Denmark, in 1891, Britain, in 1908, Australia, in 1909 and America in 1935. The German scheme was a social insurance scheme, which provided workers with invalidity benefits up to age 70, and an old age pension thereafter. Contributions were compulsory, and, like pension benefits, were graduated in line with earnings from employment. By linking pension benefits to earnings, the scheme ensured that the best-paid workers would also have the highest incomes in retirement. Thane (2000) notes that the motivation for the introduction of the German scheme had as much to do with containing socialism as it did with alleviating poverty amongst the old. By favouring better-off workers, who tended to support the socialist Social Democratic Party, the scheme was intended to show that they too could benefit from the existing political system. The scheme did little for the poorest workers. Low paid and casual male workers, along with most women, were not included.

In Britain, Canon William Blackley had proposed a system of social insurance more than a decade before the introduction of the German scheme. Blackley's proposals involved the provision of invalidity benefits for wage earners, with a flat-rate pension payable at age 70. Thus, he sought to tackle the two major causes of pauperism: sickness and old age. The scheme was to have been financed out of a fund built up from compulsory contributions made by young workers. His opponents cited two objections. The first was cost. Such a scheme would be expensive to administer. The second was the belief that social insurance would discourage personal thrift and foster dependence on the state. His opponents won the day. The scheme that was eventually introduced in Britain, under the 1908 Pensions Act, was very different from the one Blackley had advocated.

The 1908 scheme was a non-contributory one. It paid pensions – financed out of general taxation – to those aged 70 and over, whose incomes were less than 12 shillings (60p) per week. It was hardly a pension scheme at all. Rather, like the earlier Danish scheme, it was a mechanism for delivering means-tested public assistance to the elderly poor. Seventy was chosen as the qualifying age for a pension on grounds of cost. As Thane (1978) points out, at the time, it was generally agreed that 65 was actually the age at which most workers' physical powers had declined to the point where they were no longer capable of regular employment. A pension scheme based on social insurance was not introduced until the Widows', Orphans' and Old Age Contributory Pensions Act was passed in 1925. This followed the introduction of disability insurance, in 1911.

The 1925 scheme provided pensions payable as of right at age 65, in return for contributions made throughout an individual's working life. Like the scheme it replaced, the new one sought only to provide an income safety net for the elderly. Thus it maintained the practice of paying flat-rate retirement benefits. Not all workers were covered, though; only hourly-paid workers in a narrow range of industries were required to join the scheme. In a series of reforms culminating in the National Insurance Act of 1946, however, coverage was extended to the point where participation became virtually universal, and the retirement age for women was reduced to 60.

A second scheme – the graduated pension scheme (GPS) – was established in 1961. The intention was to introduce a measure of income maintenance into Britain's public pension arrangements. The GPS was an earnings-related supplementary state pension. In return for additional National Insurance contributions, graduated according to income, workers could build up entitlements to an earnings-related top-up to the basic state pension. In 1971, however, the government proposed scrapping the GPS, which was ultimately replaced, in 1975, with the state earnings-related pension scheme (SERPS). Though short-lived, the GPS established the first formal link between state and private pension provision in the UK. A worker could opt out of the GPS if his or her employer provided an occupational scheme offering equivalent or better benefits – a process known as non-participation.

SERPS, like the GPS, provides an earnings-related top-up to the basic state pension. Membership is compulsory for all but the lowest paid workers, although, as with the GPS, employees can opt out of SERPS if they are contributing to a contracted-out occupational scheme or an approved personal pension plan. Unlike the GPS, with its system of graduated contributions, entitlement to a pension from SERPS is based upon a uniform contribution rate for participating workers and their employers. In its original form, SERPS was intended to provide pension benefits worth 25 per cent of a worker's earnings between a lower and an upper limit, averaged over their best 20 years. Concerns about the cost of SERPS, though, led the Government to postpone full implementation of the scheme until 1998. Anyone retiring before this date would receive a much less generous earnings-related state pension.

The existence of public pensions can be justified on a number of grounds. The first of these is the alleviation of poverty in old age. In an ideal world, there would be no need for public pensions. Individuals would save throughout their working lives and live off their savings during retirement. In reality, though, some people will have incomes which are too low to permit them to save enough during their working lives to ensure that they have an adequate standard of living in retirement. Thus, there is a *prima facie* case for compulsory income redistribution to provide these individuals with minimum retirement incomes. As Dilnot *et al.* (1994) point out, the provision of guaranteed pensions through a systematic redistribution of income from the rich to the poor can only be undertaken by the state, or under the direction of the state.

Public pensions can also be justified on grounds of paternalism and the need to prevent free-riding. The case for paternalism rests on the belief that individuals do not always act in their own best interests. People are often short-sighted, valuing the relative certainty of immediate consumption more highly than the less certain prospect of consuming in the future. Left to themselves, then, working-age people will frequently fail to save enough for their retirement, even when they can afford to do so. By forcing them to save for retirement, public pensions protect people from the adverse consequences of their own myopic or feckless tendencies.

Free-riding can occur where society is unwilling to allow people to live out their old age in penury. The willingness of taxpayers to support the elderly poor will diminish people's incentive to make their own provision for retirement. Moreover, some people may seek to maximise their lifetime consumption by deliberately consuming their entire incomes before retirement in the knowledge that taxpayers will ensure that they have enough to live on for the rest of their lives. The more generous society is to the destitute poor, the greater will be the incentive for some people to free-ride. By forcing individuals to save for retirement, public pensions protect taxpayers against free-riders.

While paternalism and the need to prevent free-riding provide a rationale for compulsory saving for retirement, they do not, by themselves, represent a justification for public pensions. People could be compelled to save privately with commercial pension providers – as they are in Chile – or, as in Australia, be required to participate in employer-provided pension schemes. Public pensions may be desirable, though, if they allow governments to achieve their paternalistic objectives and prevent free-riding more efficiently than would be possible with compulsory private saving for retirement. Because they avoid the need for expensive marketing and benefit from economies of scale, public pensions can be provided at lower administrative cost than is possible with private sector schemes. In addition, public pensions will clearly be desirable in countries where the institutions required for private saving – well-functioning capital and insurance markets, for example – are either absent or underdeveloped.

Although a strong theoretical case exists for redistributive public pensions, it is less clear whether these should be available to all retired people – the universal approach – or restricted to those with the greatest need – the targeted approach. As Section 1.1 shows, public pensions are not the only form of income available to those over retirement age. Income from employment, investments, occupational and personal pensions means that considerable differences exist in the incomes received by elderly people. Universality makes sense when the vast majority of retired people are poor. This was undoubtedly the situation at the time when public pensions were first introduced, but it is not the case today. Targeting pension benefits on those who need them most might, therefore, make more sense where significant inequalities exist in the incomes and wealth of retired people.

A compelling argument for targeting can be made on both moral and cost grounds. Redistribution necessarily involves making some people worse off in order to make others better off. It is arguably wrong, though, to tax working people, many of whom will be struggling to pay off mortgages and raise families, simply to pay pensions to retired people who already have sufficient income from other sources. A means test should, therefore, be employed to identify those in genuine need of a state pension. Retired people with incomes above some threshold level – say 50 per cent of average earnings – might be entitled to reduced pensions, whilst those with very high alternative incomes might have their entitlement to a state pension withdrawn altogether. Targeting would thus ensure that generous benefits could be paid to the poorest pensioners without imposing an excessive burden on the working population.

Whilst the moral and cost arguments for targeting public pensions are strong, means-testing may not be the best way of making sure that pension benefits only go to those who really need them. Means tests are complex and, therefore, expensive to administer. Information about applicants must be collected and processed in order to determine eligibility. The savings achieved through means-testing public pensions will thus be partially offset by the higher administrative cost of the scheme. Means tests are a fairly good way to ensure that benefits do not go to those who don't qualify for them, but are less good at ensuring that people who really need them actually get them. Some eligible individuals will fail to apply for a means-tested pension because they are not aware that they are entitled to receive one. Others will be put off if they regard the application process as demeaning or excessively complex. Consequently, take-up of means-tested benefits is always less than 100 per cent of those who are eligible to receive them.

Because means-testing discriminates against the better off, it can give rise to perverse effects on the saving and consumption behaviour of working-age individuals, and create resentment amongst different groups of retired people. This is especially true where pension benefits for those who qualify are generous. The young will have little incentive to save for their old age if their savings will ultimately disqualify them from receiving a state pension. On the contrary, they will have a positive incentive to consume the bulk of their lifetime earnings before they reach retirement age. Means-testing is likely, therefore, to result in lower levels of aggregate saving than would be achieved where entitlement to a pension was universal. Retired people whose savings are just over the qualifying threshold for a state pension are likely to feel considerable animosity towards their less thrifty contemporaries who do qualify. Means-testing may thus be the cause of a lower level of social cohesion than would exist if people were entitled to receive a state pension irrespective of their personal income and wealth.

Public pensions can be targeted on the most needy without the requirement for means-testing. In his seminal work on social security, William Beveridge advocated an approach to targeting based on contingent criteria (Beveridge 1942). Beveridge recognised that poverty tended to be most widespread among certain socio-economic groups such as the unemployed, the sick and the old. Redistributive state benefits should, therefore, be targeted on individuals who satisfied one or more of these contingent criteria. Since, as Section 1.9 shows, certain categories among the elderly tend to be the poorest (the 'old' old and women, for example), public pensions could be targeted solely on these groups. Such an approach would obviate the need for a means test, because everyone in the qualifying groups would receive a pension irrespective of their individual circumstances. It would also lack the disincentive effects that bedevil means-testing. Unfortunately, this approach would not ensure that all who needed a pension got one. This is because some members of the qualifying groups would actually be quite well-off, while some of those on the outside would be extremely poor.

Given the difficulties associated with targeting, the universal approach to public pension provision may actually be more attractive than it first appears. Universal pensions are cheaper to administer, and can achieve wider coverage, than those provided through targeted schemes. They are also less likely than means-tested pensions to provoke resentment among different groups of retired people. They may, if designed carefully, also have less of a distorting effect on individuals' saving and consumption behaviour. The redistributive nature of public pensions means that the universal approach is likely to enjoy a much higher level of public acceptance than would be the case with targeting. As Wilson (1974) suggests, even if some individuals don't need the income provided by a universal public pension, as long as there are large numbers who do, universality might still be justified on grounds of convenience.

In some countries – Australia, for example – the state's financial support for the elderly is mainly delivered on a means-tested basis. In Italy, on the other hand, public pensions are universal. The British approach – discussed more fully in Section 1.3 – comprises a mix of universality and targeting. The state provides a virtually universal basic old-age pension, the value of which is substantially below what is officially deemed to be adequate. In addition, a means-tested supplementary retirement benefit is used to deliver additional income to the poorest pensioners.

Linked to the debate about targeting versus universality is the question of generosity. What level of pension income should the state provide? Should the state's role be confined to providing retired people with a minimum level of pension income, sufficient to keep them out of poverty? On the other hand, should the state undertake to replace workers' incomes completely, or in part, once they reach retirement age? The question of generosity cannot be analysed purely in economic terms. The economic issues are important, but a proper analysis of the generosity question also involves normative judgements about the nature of society, individual responsibility and the role of the state.

Public pension schemes which provide a basic or minimum retirement income avoid some of the pitfalls associated with more generous schemes. Other things being equal, they are relatively cheap, absorbing a smaller proportion of GDP than income replacement schemes. Anyone wishing to enjoy a higher level of consumption in retirement than the minimum pension would permit will have an incentive to save for their old age through, for example, an occupational pension scheme or an individual pension plan. Thus, minimum public pensions tend to promote self-reliance and encourage people to take personal responsibility for their economic well-being in old age in a way that income replacement schemes do not. Not surprisingly, then, minimum public pensions are particularly attractive to societies which emphasise the importance of self-reliance rather than collective responsibility. Examples include America, Australia and the UK.

Because minimum public pensions usually provide flat-rate retirement benefits, their effective income replacement rates vary between individuals. For example, if the scheme provides an income replacement rate of 50 per cent of average earnings, someone with a pre-retirement income equal to 50 per cent of the average would receive a 100 per cent level of income replacement. On the other hand, someone with pre-retirement earnings 25 per cent above the average would receive an effective income replacement rate of just 40 per cent. Minimum pension schemes thus favour low-earners. This might be seen as desirable if inequalities in pre-retirement earnings are to some extent a matter of luck. Minimum public pensions will tend to reduce the differences in individuals' lifetime incomes. It can also be argued that low-income workers need a higher rate of income replacement because consumption expenditure absorbs a higher proportion of their total incomes.

Public pension systems that provide complete or partial income replacement are arguably fairer than basic income schemes. This is because they do not discriminate against workers with middle and higher earnings. If contributions are also linked to earnings, it might not matter that those with superior incomes from employment also end up with higher pensions. Indeed, as Johnson (1992) observes, it might be argued that the state should provide income-related pensions because those used to higher incomes from employment actually need relatively higher incomes in retirement. A major criticism of income replacement schemes is that they eliminate the need for personal saving for retirement, and thereby absolve individuals of the need to take responsibility for their own economic welfare in old age. This is only a weakness, though, if society values personal self-reliance more highly than collective responsibility. A more telling indictment, however, is that income replacement schemes are more expensive than basic income schemes, and perpetuate labour market inequalities into old age.

Another aspect of generosity concerns the method by which pensions are periodically increased. The need to uprate pension benefits arises because both prices and earnings tend to increase over time. If the value of pension benefits is fixed, inflation will reduce their value to current pensioners, while increases in earnings will reduce their replacement value to future pensioners. Pensioners' incomes are particularly vulnerable to erosion by inflation, since, as Turner (1998) observes, the old generally cannot re-enter the labour market in order to compensate for the negative effects of increased prices on their retirement benefits. On the other hand, workers are vulnerable to increases in average earnings if these are not matched by equivalent increases in pension benefits. If prices and earnings rose at the same rate, uprating would be straightforward. As long as pensions were increased by the same amount, both the replacement rate and the real value of pensions would remain constant over time.

In practice, earnings tend to rise faster than prices. Increasing existing pensions by the rate of inflation and raising future pension entitlements by the increase in earnings would maintain the replacement rate and preserve the real value of pensions currently in payment. Unfortunately, over time this approach to uprating would also cause significant inequalities to arise in the pension incomes of younger and older pensioners. This problem can be overcome if all pensions – current and future – are indexed either to increases in prices or to earnings growth. Applying the same method of indexation to all pensions, however, is also problematic. Linking pension increases to inflation – price uprating – will preserve the real value of current pensions, but the replacement rate for future pensioners will fall. Earnings uprating, on the other hand, whilst maintaining the replacement rate, is the most expensive method of indexation. This is because the rate of increase of current pensions would be greater than that under price uprating.

Although considerable differences exist in the design of public schemes around the world, most countries now have some form of PAYG pension arrangements. In 1995, the most common public schemes were contributory schemes providing earnings-related benefits (Turner 1998). Many countries devote a substantial part of their gross domestic product (GDP) to public pension payments. In the mid 1990s, spending on public pensions by the 15 member countries of the European Union (EU) averaged 12 per cent of GDP. Italy spent the most, 14.2 per cent, and the UK the least, 4.8 per cent. The figures for Australia, Japan and the US were 3.3 per cent, 6.6 per cent and 4.6 per cent respectively (Disney and Johnson 2001). National differences in the so-called pensions burden – the ratio of public pension payments to GDP – reflect, among other things, differences in the types of benefits provided and overall scheme generosity. In general, the greater the flat-rate component of public pensions and the lower the replacement rate – the ratio of pension payments to earned incomes – the lower the pensions burden. Pensions burdens tend to be highest in those countries where benefits are predominantly earnings-related, and where income maintenance is the central objective of the public scheme. Italy and Germany are cases in point. Both provide generous income-related public pensions – the replacement rate is nearly 70 per cent in Germany and 80 per cent in Italy.

1.3 CHANGES AND CHALLENGES

When public pensions were first established in Britain, social and economic conditions were very different from those which exist today. Far fewer people lived to be old. In 1901, average life expectancy at birth was just 51 for men and 58 for women (Thane 2000). High birth rates and low life expectancy meant that the number of elderly people in the population represented a small fraction of the total. Most old people were poor, compared with those of working age. For most workers, public pensions were their only insurance against an impoverished old age. What is more, public pensions were a relatively cheap form of old-age insurance, because the cost of providing pensions for a relatively small group of retired people was spread over a much larger number of workers. Indeed, retired people could actually receive more in pension benefits than they had paid in contributions.

Average life expectancy is now 76 for men and nearly 81 for women. Consequently, more people than ever are living to retirement age, and those who do are also living longer in retirement. Fertility – the average number of children born to each woman – is, however, much lower than it used to be. The reasons for these changes in life expectancy and fertility are discussed in Section 1.4. Together, greater longevity and lower fertility have altered the population balance between young and old. Not only do older people now represent a much larger share of the total population, the old-age dependency ratio – the ratio of pensioners to workers – has increased significantly. Moreover, this ageing of the population is forecast to continue. As Table 1.3.1 shows, in Britain and other countries the ratio of people aged 60 and over to those aged 20-59 is projected to rise sharply in the next two decades.

The phenomenon of population ageing has motivated governments around the world to introduce reforms aimed at preventing public pension costs from spiralling out of control and placing an intolerable burden on workers and their employers. Some have gone further than others. In the United States and the Republic of Ireland, an element of prefunding has been introduced into public pensions. In the US, workers' pension contributions and those of their employers are no longer used exclusively to pay the current pensions bill. Instead, a small portion of all contributions is accumulated in an OASDI trust fund from which part of the future pensions bill will be paid. America, like some other countries, has also raised its state pension age – the age at which individuals become entitled to receive public pension payments. Chile and Mexico have closed their public pension schemes to young workers, and introduced a system of compulsory private saving for retirement. Some other Latin-American countries have introduced compulsory private saving for retirement in addition to public pensions. Australia has done something very similar.

In Ireland, the decision to part-fund future public pension expenditures was part of a package of reforms arising from a National Pensions Policy Initiative begun in 1996. Although demographic conditions in Ireland are more favourable than in many other countries, and are projected to remain so, public pension expenditures are forecast to rise substantially after 2025. The National Pensions Reserve Fund (NPRF) was launched on

Table 1.3.1 Projected change in the ratio of people aged 60 and over to those aged 20–59 in selected countries, 2000 and 2025

	2000	*2025*	*Percentage change*
Argentina	0.28	0.34	21.4
Australia	0.30	0.50	66.7
Austria	0.36	0.59	63.9
Belgium	0.35	0.56	60.0
Brazil	0.15	0.28	86.7
Canada	0.29	0.54	86.2
Chile	0.20	0.37	85.0
China	0.18	0.35	94.4
Denmark	0.35	0.56	60.0
Finland	0.36	0.64	77.8
France	0.38	0.58	52.6
Germany	0.41	0.62	51.2
Greece	0.42	0.59	40.5
Hungary	0.35	0.50	42.9
Iceland	0.28	0.51	82.1
India	0.14	0.21	50.0
Ireland	0.28	0.43	53.6
Italy	0.42	0.65	54.8
Japan	0.41	0.69	68.3
Luxembourg	0.35	0.46	31.4
Mexico	0.13	0.23	76.9
Netherlands	0.32	0.57	78.1
New Zealand	0.28	0.40	42.9
Norway	0.35	0.53	51.4
Poland	0.30	0.50	66.7
Portugal	0.37	0.52	40.5
Romania	0.34	0.42	23.5
Russia	0.34	0.48	41.2
Spain	0.38	0.59	55.3
Sweden	0.41	0.61	48.8
UK	0.38	0.56	47.4

Source: US Census Bureau, Summary Demographic Indicators, International Database, 2001.

2 April 2001, to receive an annual sum from general government revenues equal to 1 per cent of GNP. It is administered by an independent NPRF Commission made up of seven Commissioners. The NPRF Commission, which is accountable to the Minister for Finance and the Irish Parliament, is responsible for setting the fund's investment strategy and appointing a fund manager.

Unlike America's OASDI trust fund, which was set up in the 1980s and which invests exclusively in US government bonds, the NPRF is prohibited from holding Irish government securities. This is to ensure that the fund cannot be used to provide the Irish government with a guaranteed market for its debt. The NPRF Commission must pursue a strictly commercial investment strategy aimed at securing the best possible long-term returns. The potential exists for a large investor like the NPRF to influence the governance of the firms in which it invests. For this reason, there are limits on the size of NPRF investments in individual companies, to prevent the fund from gaining a controlling interest. Contributions to public pension expenditures from the NPRF are not permitted before 2025.

For more than 20 years, the approach to pensions reform in Britain has comprised three elements. These are pension benefit cuts, greater reliance on private pensions and means-testing. Since 1980, the basic state pension has only been increased each year in line with inflation. This exclusive use of price uprating contrasts with the former practice of raising pension benefits annually in line with increases in either prices or average earnings, whichever was the greater. As noted in Section 1.2, the effect of price uprating is to preserve the real worth of the basic pension, but, over time, to reduce its value relative to earned incomes. This is because earnings from employment normally rise faster than prices. The basic state pension is currently worth around 15 per cent of average male earnings, compared with 20 per cent in 1981.

Benefits from SERPS have also been cut. Under a new, less generous, benefits formula introduced in the mid-1980s, the value of pensions from SERPS was cut to 20 per cent of eligible earnings averaged over 40 years. Then, in 1995, a much less generous method of uprating benefits from SERPS was introduced. Widows' benefits have also been cut. Before April 2000, widows could inherit their deceased husbands' SERPS pension in full, whereas now they are entitled to receive just half. As of April 2003, SERPS is being phased out and replaced with a new scheme, the State Second Pension (S2P). Participation in the new scheme will be restricted to low-paid workers, although the benefits provided will be superior to those they could have obtained through SERPS.

For women, public pension benefits are set to fall further as a result of a decision, taken in the early 1990s, to equalise male and female retirement ages. From 2010, the state pension age for women will be 65 rather than 60. This five-year reduction in the pensionable portion of womens' lives will shave billions of pounds off the annual pensions bill. The change will be phased in over a ten-year period. Women born before 6 April 1950 will be unaffected. The retirement age for a woman born between 6 April 1950 and 5 April 1955 will be between 60 and 65, depending upon her date of birth. All women born on or after 6 April 1955 will have to wait until they are 65 before they can collect their state pensions.

By the 1980s, it was no longer the case that all pensioners were poor. Many of those entering retirement had substantial private resources. Several decades of rapid earnings growth and participation in employer-provided pension schemes allowed many people to retire with large amounts of personal savings and good occupational pension incomes. In addition, many had considerable housing wealth, the result of the post-war boom in home ownership. The Conservative governments of the day regarded this increase in private retirement resources as something that could, and should, be encouraged. Private provision for retirement could fill the pensions gap that would result from reductions in public pension benefits. Just as important, the idea that individuals should accumulate their own private retirement nest eggs fitted the Conservative philosophy of free enterprise and self-reliance. In 1986, legislation was passed which made it possible for workers who were not members of a contracted-out occupational scheme to leave SERPS and contribute instead to individual schemes known as Personal Pension Plans. More recently, a Labour government has sought to extend personal saving for retirement, with the introduction, in 2001, of Stakeholder Pensions.

For those with little or no private retirement income, means-tested social security top-ups have been, and will continue to be, used to fill the gap left by cuts in public pension benefits. By the late 1980s, the value of the basic state pension had fallen below the income ceiling for means-tested income support. In April 2001, the ceiling for the Minimum Income Guarantee (MIG) – the new name for pensioners' income support – was some 27 per cent above the value of the BSP for single pensioners and 21 per cent higher for couples. In 2000, 627,000 claimants over state pension age were receiving MIG payments (ONS 2002; Table 1.3.2). As Falkingham and Rake (2001) observe, means-tested benefits, rather than the BSP, are now the principle mechanism for ensuring the adequacy of retirement incomes in the UK. Moreover, the gap between the MIG ceiling and the basic pension will gradually widen, since the MIG, unlike the basic pension, is to be increased each year in line with earnings growth. The State Second Pension and a pension credit, both introduced in 2003, will further extend the role of means-testing in the UK's public pension arrangements.

Governments and non-governmental organisations around the world are increasingly relying on generational accounting to estimate the long-term costs arising from population ageing. Generational accounting is a technique developed in the 1990s (Kotlikoff 1992, Auerbach *et al.*, 1994) which measures the tax burden for future generations implied by current fiscal policy. In preparing a set of generational accounts for the UK,

Table 1.3.2 Claimants of state pension age by key benefit type in 2000

Benefit type	Claimants
Sick and disabled	2,530,000
Non-disabled income support (MIG)	627,000
Retirement pension only	7,367,000

Source: ONS 2002.

Cardarelli *et al.* (1999) found that, partly as a result of its pension reforms, Britain was in a better position to meet the challenge of population ageing than Japan, the US and some other European countries. It is unlikely, though, that the implementation of the reforms planned for 2003 will mark the end of public pension reform in Britain.

1.4 POPULATION AGEING IN BRITAIN

The average age of people living in Britain is projected to rise from around 38, as it is today, to 44 in 2041, as the share of the population aged 60 and over rises. As Figure 1.4.1 shows, the population share of people aged 60 and over is forecast to rise from 20 per cent in 2001 to 30 per cent in 2030, and to 31 per cent by 2050. The support ratio – the number of workers for every state pensioner – is projected to fall from 3.4 in 2001 to 2.4 in 2041 (Figure 1.4.2), as the old age dependency ratio rises (Figure 1.4.3). These projections are based upon actual changes in life expectancy, fertility and net migration which took place during the second half of the twentieth-century – discussed below – and upon assumptions about the paths these variables will take in the future (this is discussed in detail in Dunnell 2000).

Between 1951 and 1999, average life expectancy at birth rose by 9.8 years for a man and 9.6 years for a woman. Much of this increase in life expectancy was due to improvements in survival rates among the young. The success of mass immunisation programmes aimed at a range of infectious diseases meant that large numbers of children and young adults were no longer dying each year from conditions like measles, diphtheria and

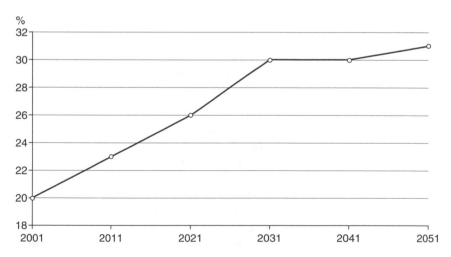

Figure 1.4.1 Projected change in the population share of people aged 60 and over, UK 2001–2051 (Dunnell (2000)).

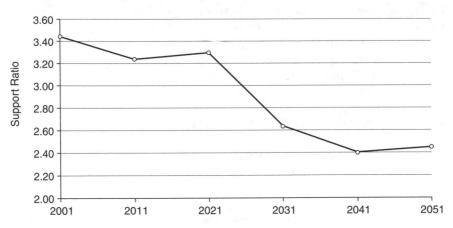

Figure 1.4.2 Projected change in the support ratio, UK 2001–2051 (Dunnell (2000)).

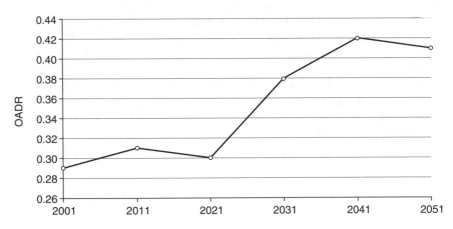

Figure 1.4.3 Projected change in the old age dependency ratio (OADR), UK 2001–2051 (Dunnell (2000)).

tuberculosis. Medical advances and improvements in neo-natal care dramatically reduced the infant mortality rate (the number of deaths occurring each year among children under 1). As Table 1.4.1 shows, between 1970 and 1996 infant mortality fell from 18.5 deaths per thousand live births to just 6 per thousand. Reductions in workplace fatalities and improvements in the general health of the workforce also meant that increases in the number of children surviving to adulthood were accompanied by substantial improvements in survival rates amongst people of working age. By the mid-1990s, only 1 in 10 individuals who survived to 16 died before reaching the age of 65.

Table 1.4.1 Infant mortality rates, UK 1970–2000

	1970	1980	1990	1996	2000*
Deaths in first year per 1, 000 live births	18.5	12.1	7.9	6.0	6.0

Source: Council of Europe (1998).

Note
* US Census Bureau Summary Demographic Indicators, International Database (2001).

From the 1960s, survival rates amongst older age groups also began to increase. What is more, this upward trend in the life expectancy of older age groups accelerated in the 1980s, as medical advances, better diet and greater public awareness of the benefits of a healthier life-style began to reduce the number of deaths from heart disease, strokes, cancers and other killer conditions affecting the elderly. Improvements in survival rates amongst older age groups are reflected in the numbers of people living to 100 or more: in 1951 there were 300 centenarians in the UK, and by 2001 there were more than 8,000. Today's very low rates of mortality amongst children and working-age people mean that, in the future, increases in average life expectancy will come mainly from further improvements in the survival rates of the elderly.

Changes in the pattern of fertility during the second half of the twentieth century contrast with the steady upward trend in life expectancy observed over the period. The annual number of births turned sharply upwards after 1956, and continued rising until 1964. This baby boom, which added an extra three million people to the population of Great Britain, was followed by a sustained downward trend in fertility. The average number of children born to women in the baby boom years was around 2.5. It fell to around 2.1 children per woman in the early 1970s, and is now about 1.8. A feature of this decline in fertility was a reduction in the numbers of children born to older women. Motherhood became the preoccupation of the young, as women increasingly chose to complete their families in their mid- to late-twenties.

Since the early 1990s, UK net migration – the number of immigrants minus the number of emigrants – has been rather high, at over 100,000 per annum. At other times it has been low or negative. For example, Jackson (1998) notes that the number of emigrants marginally exceeded the number of immigrants over the period 1945–1970. Primary immigration – the permanent resettlement of foreign workers and their families – declined during the 1960s and 1970s, following the introduction of a series of restrictions beginning with the 1962 Commonwealth Immigrants Act. The majority of immigrants to Britain in the 1980s and early 1990s were dependants of those already resident in the country. The high net migration of recent years is mainly due to a substantial increase in the number of asylum applications and an easing of immigration rules in the late 1990s. Overall, the effect of changes in net migration on the size and age distribution of Britain's population has been rather small, compared with the effect of changes in life expectancy and fertility.

1.5 OCCUPATIONAL PENSIONS

Occupational pension schemes pre-date public pensions. A distinction can be made between company schemes which are sponsored by a single employer, and industry-wide schemes established by groups of employers. In some countries, most notably Germany and Japan, occupational schemes often provide retired employees with pensions financed on a PAYG basis. The weekly or monthly pensions bill is met from the operating revenues of the company. By contrast, in the UK and America, occupational schemes are almost always funded. Instead of paying someone else's pension, employees and/or their employers make contributions to a fund which is used to provide them with a pension when they retire.

A distinction can also be made between DB and DC occupational schemes. In a DB scheme, the level of pension income a retiring worker can expect to receive is predetermined by the rules of the scheme. Typically, DB schemes offer a level of pension income calculated as a fixed fraction – e.g. a sixtieth or an eightieth – of an employee's final or average salary, multiplied by years of service. Thus, workers accruing one-sixtieth of their final salary would receive a pension equal to two-thirds of their earnings after 40 years of service. Workers who leave a DB scheme early can either transfer their accrued entitlements to another occupational scheme, or have them preserved until they reach retirement age. Preserved pensions must be increased annually in line with inflation, up to a maximum of 5 per cent, to preserve their real value. Unlike DC schemes, which are always funded, DB schemes can be financed on either a funded or a PAYG basis.

The difference between DB and DC schemes lies in the nature of the employer's pension commitment, and in the link between contributions made and benefits received. DB schemes are based on an employer's promise to provide retiring workers with a specific level of income. If the assets of the scheme are insufficient to meet this promise, the employer must make up the shortfall. Thus, there is no direct link between the amount of money contributed by workers and the pension incomes they receive. DC schemes, on the other hand, do not incorporate an employer's benefit pledge. Instead, employers simply undertake to make contributions, along with their employees, to a pension fund which is invested for growth. Each worker's share of the fund – contributions plus investment returns – is used to buy him or her an annuity on retirement. Contributions and benefits are linked, because the more a worker contributes, the bigger the annuity that can be purchased at retirement.

DC schemes are front-loaded, because, due to the compounding of investment returns, the amount of pension income generated by each contribution is less than that generated by the previous one. Early contributions are, therefore, worth much more than those made later on. DB schemes, on the other hand, are back-loaded. Since pension values are a function of earnings – which rise over time – and length of service, early contributions generate smaller amounts of pension income than those made later on. Both types of scheme are especially advantageous for workers who join early and maintain their membership right up to retirement age.

In 2002, around 42 million Americans had some pension savings in so-called 401(k) plans. Employee and employer contributions to these DC occupational schemes are tax free. Moreover, workers have a choice about how much to save each month and how their 401(k) savings are invested. Following the collapse of the US energy firm Enron (discussed in Section 2.7), concerns have been expressed about the very high proportions of 401(k) investments that are typically held in the shares of the sponsoring company. An important difference between UK occupational DC schemes and 401(k) plans is the ability of 401(k) planholders to make 'hardship withdrawals' and to cash-out their savings when they change employers, subject to a 10 per cent rate of taxation.

In Britain, occupational pension schemes were first established for government servants, in the early eighteenth century. Although entitlement to a pension had to be earned, it was not automatic. There was no formal retirement age, and pensions were awarded at the discretion of the Civil Service Commissioners. Pensions were only granted to those with a record of exemplary service who were, by dint of age, no longer able to perform their duties effectively. By the 1830s, however, all civil servants had the right to retire with a salary-related pension at age 60. The civil service scheme formed the model for other public sector schemes, like the teachers' and local government employees' schemes, introduced towards the end of the nineteenth century.

Before the emergence of civil service pensions, it had been usual for retiring officials to secure a form of pension by selling their offices to their successors. They would do so for either a lump sum or an annuity, paid for out of their successor's salary. As a reward for loyal service, daily-paid and lower-ranking employees were often given small *ex gratia* pensions when they got too old to work. *Ex gratia* payments to former workers were also common in the private sector, where occupational schemes were slower to emerge. In addition, employers frequently took care of their older workers by transferring them to lighter duties, such as carrying messages, gate-keeping or sweeping up, rather than dismissing them altogether.

By the 1890s, private sector occupational schemes were present in the mining, railway and banking industries. Many large manufacturing firms also had their own pension schemes. Occupational schemes were less widespread among small firms. In common with the early civil service schemes, employers had a veto on the granting of pensions. Strikers and other trouble-makers were frequently denied a pension, and thus the pension scheme could be used as a tool for ensuring a loyal and compliant workforce. By the 1920s, though, most occupational schemes had evolved into a form we would recognise today, with a formal retirement age and an automatic right to a salary-related pension linked to years of service. In 1936, around 1.5 million private sector workers were members of an occupational scheme (Occupational Pensions Board 1997).

Until the 1970s, it was common for private sector employers to operate differential pensions policies. While their white-collar employees were provided with salary-related DB pensions, blue-collar workers were placed in money purchase schemes. Problems emerged in the 1970s, though, when a combination of low investment returns and rampant inflation caused members of money purchase schemes to lose out, while those in DB schemes had their pension entitlements protected by increased employer contributions. Although many employers responded by introducing DB schemes for all employees, this did not mean that workers were treated equally. The accrual rate for blue-collar workers was frequently set at one-eightieth per year of service, compared with one-sixtieth for white-collar staff.

As Table 1.5.1 shows, membership of occupational pension schemes expanded rapidly in the two decades after World War II, and reached a peak in 1983. Thereafter, membership contracted somewhat. According to the Government Actuary's eleventh survey of occupational schemes, in 2000 around 10.1 million workers – considerably less than half of all employees – were members of public and private sector occupational schemes (GAD 2003). Coverage was much greater among public sector workers than it was amongst employees in the private sector. Those actually receiving occupational pensions numbered 8.2 million – 5.2 million from private sector schemes and 3 million from public sector schemes. Whereas almost all schemes in the public sector were of the DB type, a variety of arrangements could be found in the private sector. Of the estimated 151,000 private schemes then in operation, around 38,000 were DB schemes and 109,500 were of the DC type. The remaining 3,500 schemes were hybrids, having an element of both defined benefit and defined contribution.

Considerable differences exist in the form and extent of occupational pension provision in the member countries of the OECD (Davis 1995). In terms of their similarity to the situation in Britain, occupational pension arrangements in Canada and the United States are the closest. There is a mix of employer-provided defined benefit and money purchase schemes, although the option to contract out of the public scheme is not available in America and Canada. As in Britain, public sector workers have a higher level of coverage compared with private sector employees. Women benefit

Table 1.5.1 Percentage of employees covered by an occupational pension scheme, 1953–1995

	Men	Women	All
1953	34	18	28
1963	63	21	48
1971	62	28	49
1983	64	37	52
1987	60	35	49
1991	57	37	48
1995*	52	39	46

Source: Sullivan (1996a).

Note
* GAD 10th Survey of Occupational Pension Schemes.

less than men from occupational schemes, and have lower rates of participation. Whereas the provision of occupational pensions is voluntary in Canada, the US and Great Britain, it is mandatory in Australia. Moreover, Australian schemes are money purchase plans providing lump sum retirement benefits which may or may not be annuitised. In Europe, Germany and the Scandinavian countries have extensive occupational pension provision. By contrast, in Greece and Italy the existence of very generous public schemes has served to discourage the development of occupational pension schemes.

Most UK occupational pension schemes are established as trust funds, under legislation passed in 1927 (Blake 1992). Scheme assets are separate from those of the sponsoring employer – or employers in the case of multi-employer schemes – and are held in trust for members by a board of trustees. Under UK common law, trustees have a fiduciary duty to act in the best interests of scheme beneficiaries. Although trust law was originally a means of ensuring that endowments for widows and orphans were managed correctly (Davis 2001), it is regarded by many as the most appropriate way to protect members of occupational schemes from the insolvency or default of sponsors. A perceived lack of trustee independence, however, has led others to question the appropriateness of applying trust law to occupational pensions.

Trustees are appointed by schemes' sponsoring companies, and are in turn responsible for appointing scheme actuaries and auditors. They set out in writing the investment principles to be followed by their scheme's fund managers. As Section 2.6 notes, since the implementation of the 1995 Pensions Act, trustees may be fined and disqualified for breaching the rules under which they operate. A scheme's actuaries and auditors are not permitted to act as its trustees. In addition, individuals who are (or have been) bankrupt, have been convicted of an offence of deception or dishonesty, or are disqualified company directors may not serve as trustees. Since

1997, at least one third of trustee board members must be elected by scheme beneficiaries.

For employers, funding occupational pensions has a number of advantages over PAYG financing. Not the least of these is tax relief available to sponsoring firms on contributions they make to their pension funds. In the case of DB schemes, the amount of money employers must contribute in order to finance their pension obligations is reduced by the investment returns earned by their schemes, which are also largely free of taxation. Funding can also generate a valuable source of external finance, since sponsors may benefit from an equity investment by, or receive a loan from, their pension schemes. In the past, the absence of a firm's pensions liabilities from its books could benefit its credit rating, thereby reducing its borrowing costs.

Employers are required by law to ensure that their DB schemes have sufficient funds available to meet their pension obligations. Because the amounts workers contribute cannot generally be altered – being specified by the rules of their schemes – employers must make good any shortfalls that are identified by their scheme actuaries. Shortfalls arise when contributions are inadequate. This situation can occur when investment returns are low and/or workers' pension entitlements are rising rapidly. On the other hand, when investment returns are high and/or pension commitments are rising slowly – or even falling – contributions may be too high. In this case DB schemes can accumulate financial surpluses. For employers, the potential to utilise scheme surpluses for their own purposes represents another important benefit of funding over PAYG financing.

The day-to-day management of occupational pension fund assets can be carried out in several ways. One way is for sponsors to invest their pension funds directly. To do this, sponsors either use their own in-house fund managers, or they employ a specialist fund management firm to act on their behalf. Funds can also be managed on an insured basis. In this case, the fund management task is transferred to an insurance company. Purchasing the services of a specialist fund management firm, or employing in-house fund managers, is expensive. Consequently, only the largest occupational funds tend to be managed directly. The assets of small and medium-sized funds are usually managed on an insured basis, either individually or, as is often the case with small schemes, pooled with the assets of several other pension funds. In 2001, £710 billion of occupational pension scheme funds was being managed on a self-administered basis, and £205 billion was invested in schemes administered by insurance companies (Stears 2003).

Although trustees decide the investment aims of their schemes, and are obliged to set them out in regular SIPs – statements of investment principles – their choices are constrained by legal as well as practical considerations. The requirement for trustees to act prudently, in the best interests of scheme beneficiaries, implies that they should take proper advice, and that funds are allocated to the most appropriate assets. Prudence also dictates that, consistent with the needs of their schemes, trustees should select investment portfolios which are well diversified both across and within different asset classes. In general, mature schemes – ones where pension liabilities are high relative to income – need to contain a higher proportion of bonds and other assets which yield a stable flow of income than of immature ones.

Among the asset classes that may be included in occupational scheme portfolios are cash, equities (company shares), fixed interest and index-linked bonds, property, and collectibles such as precious metals, antiques and works of art. Trustees will seek to match their holdings of different assets with the liabilities of their schemes, namely pensions in payment, deferred pensions of former employees and the accrued entitlements of current workers. Cash and bonds will be selected to cover immediate pension payments and the entitlements of current and former employees who are close to retirement age. Equities, which can deliver higher but less certain returns over time than cash or bonds, will be used to cover the entitlements of younger workers. Property can generate rental income for meeting immediate expenditures and capital gains for covering longer-term liabilities. Because collectibles can yield capital gains but produce no income, they are only suitable for matching medium to long-term liabilities.

The recent funding problems experienced by numerous occupational DB schemes in the UK – discussed in Section 1.7 – have been blamed, in part, on an absence of trustee independence and trustees' frequent lack of relevant skills. The argument is that trustees are frequently pressurised, for fear of dismissal, into appointing auditors, actuaries and other scheme advisors whom sponsors want to see appointed. These are advisors who tell sponsors what they want to hear, which may not necessarily accord with the long term interests of scheme beneficiaries. In addition, in a report for the government, discussed in Section 2.8, the Myners Committee found that more than 60 per cent of trustees had no formal qualifications in finance or investment, and more than two-thirds received two days or less of training. Around half of all trustees spent no more than three hours in preparation for meetings at which investment matters were discussed.

Completely separating the administration of occupational pension schemes from their sponsoring employers would be a way of ensuring trustee independence. It would also make it impossible for employers to misappropriate beneficiaries' funds, as happened in the Maxwell case discussed in Section 2.6. Schemes could, for example, be run by legally independent trust companies. In this case, the role of sponsoring employers would be confined to handing over both their own and their employees' pension contributions. The trust company would be free to choose the most efficient investment strategy for delivering scheme benefits. Problems could still emerge, however, due to conflicts of interest arising from competition between trust companies for pension scheme business. In order to keep costs down for employers, trust companies might select investment strategies aimed at generating short-term surpluses and, in doing so, expose members of DB schemes to excessive investment risk.

As noted in Section 1.1, income from occupational pensions accounts for more than a quarter of the gross incomes of UK pensioner units. In 2001–2002, 60 per cent of all pensioner units received an occupational pension income worth an average £117 per week (DWP 2003). The benefits of occupational scheme membership are not the same for everyone, however. It was noted earlier that, whether defined benefit or defined contribution, occupational schemes work best for those with long and uninterrupted careers. Late joiners, early leavers and workers with discontinuous employment patterns all do less well out of occupational schemes. Because women are more likely than men to take time out of employment to raise children or care for sick or elderly relatives, they tend, on average, to have lower occupational pension incomes.

Even workers who experience life-long and continuous employment can end up doing rather badly out of occupational pensions. This is because DB occupational pensions are frequently subject to portability losses when workers move between employers. Workers who leave an employer's DB scheme can have their accrued pension rights preserved. Alternatively, they can receive a sum equivalent to the cash value of their accrued rights, which can be transferred into a DC plan or used to purchase service credits in another employer's DB scheme. Although preserved pensions are increased annually in line with price rises, for those who remain with the same scheme accrued entitlements are uprated at the normally higher rate of growth of real wages. Likewise, a year of service credit in a new scheme will typically cost more than the cash value of one year's accrued rights in an old scheme.

Frequent job-changers can also lose out due to the existence of vesting periods. It is usual for schemes to require a minimum period of membership – the legal maximum in the UK is two years – before employees become eligible to receive the pension rights earned by their contributions. Blake (2000) puts the size of portability losses at between 25 and 30 per cent for an individual whose employment experience involves six job changes, compared with the pension received by someone else with the same earnings who remains with one employer throughout his or her working life. A single job change can result in a portability loss of up to 16 per cent. Only workers who move between employers who participate in a sector-wide scheme are immune from portability losses.

Since 1986, members of occupational pension schemes have been permitted to make additional voluntary contributions (AVCs). AVCs allow a worker to buy additional pension benefits by contributing to a money purchase plan which runs alongside their existing occupational scheme. Although AVCs make it possible for late joiners and other workers to boost their occupational pension incomes, they cannot be used to increase lump sum payments. A weakness of AVCs, though, is that, like accrued pension rights in DB schemes, they are not fully portable. Since 1987, however, workers have had the option to make free-standing additional voluntary contributions (FSAVCs) to a DC plan which is separate from their occupational scheme and which is, therefore, portable between employers.

In 2000, around 81 per cent of occupational scheme members were in contracted-out schemes (GAD 2003). The amounts contributed to occupational schemes varied amongst employees and employers and between scheme types. Employee contributions to private sector DB schemes were mostly in the range 5 to 7 per cent of earnings. For DC schemes, the range was 2 to 4 per cent. Employers contributed much more. Employer contributions to contracted-out DB schemes were most commonly in the range 10 to 15 per cent of earnings. Where the scheme was of the DC type, employer contributions were, in most cases, less than 8 per cent of earnings. Around 10 per cent of employees who were contributing to a private sector occupational scheme were also making AVC payments. The amounts contributed to occupational schemes in the public sector are discussed in the next section.

1.6 PUBLIC SECTOR PENSIONS

It was noted in Section 1.5 that occupational pensions developed first in the public sector. The model they provided was later taken up by private sector employers. Until the late eighteenth century, the service of the state had always been performed by well-placed individuals who sought to profit personally from their official positions. Public offices were traded like commodities, and the taking of bribes and theft of government property and revenues was an everyday occurrence. As Sass (1997) and Thane (2000) show, pensions played a crucial role in the creation of the modern governmental apparatus. The establishment of career paths, with promotion based on ability and experience, ending in retirement with a good pension made public service attractive to honest and able individuals who lacked the social attributes – wealth and personal connections – traditionally required for appointment to the service of the state. Thus, pensions helped stamp out inefficiency and corruption and turn government service into an efficient, professional activity.

For employees, UK public sector schemes – like those in many other countries – are much more advantageous than the typical private sector scheme. They are mainly of the defined benefit type. Contributions are lower or non-existent, total benefits are higher, retirement occurs at an earlier age and scheme security is greater. More than four million workers are currently building up pension rights in a range of public sector schemes. Moreover, the participation rate among public sector employees in general is more than twice that of workers in the private sector. Amongst women the difference is greater still.

Public sector schemes usually provide retiring workers with tax-free lump sums equal to 3/80 of their salary for each year of service. Members of the British armed services are not required to contribute anything to their pension scheme. Although other public sector employees do make contributions, the contribution rate is often substantially below that required from workers in equivalent private sector schemes. For example, civil servants recruited since October 2002 must contribute 3 per cent of their salaries. Those in post before October 2002 make contributions of just 1.5 per cent. The average level of employee contributions to equivalent private sector schemes is around 5 per cent. At 11 per cent of pay, police officers and firefighters have the highest pension contributions of all public sector workers. On the other hand, their pension benefits accumulate at a faster rate. Entitlement to the maximum pension is earned after 30 years, compared with 40 years for other public servants.

Most public sector schemes permit retirement at 60 or younger. The typical retirement age for private sector schemes is 65. Nurses are often able to retire from the National Health Service at age 55. The faster accrual rate of police and fire service pensions means that police officers can retire at age 48 and firefighters at 50. In practice, large numbers of public sector workers are able to retire before their scheme's normal retirement age, because of very generous provisions for early retirement on health grounds. The government has expressed concern about the higher rates of early retirement on grounds of ill health amongst public sector employees. Around 40 per cent of police officers, for example, take early retirement on health grounds. Gross expenditure on public sector pensions was some £22 billion in 2002.

Because they pay benefits for longer, due to their lower retirement ages, public sector schemes provide more valuable pensions than those received from typical schemes in the private sector. In addition, public sector pensions are fully inflation-proofed. By contrast, private sector schemes are only obliged to provide inflation-proofing up to 5 per cent. The generosity of public sector schemes is usually justified on the grounds that public sector pay is relatively low compared with rates of remuneration in the private sector. In 2002–2003, pay rates in the public sector were on average 5.2 per cent below private sector rates. By accepting a job in the public sector, workers effectively trade lower current incomes for higher incomes in the future. Such a trade-off would not be possible, however, if pension promises were not secure. In fact, public sector schemes offer the most secure pension promises of all.

The overwhelming majority of UK public sector schemes are financed on a PAYG basis. The scheme for local government workers is the only major funded scheme. Unlike funded schemes, the ability of PAYG schemes to meet their pension promises is unaffected by asset market conditions. Thus, the vast majority of public sector schemes are immune to the funding problems (discussed in Section 1.7) that have led numerous private sector employers to cease providing defined benefit pensions. Even where public sector pensions are funded, workers' accrued pension rights are ultimately underwritten by the taxpayer. Because there is no fund to steal, contributors to PAYG public sector schemes are free from the risk of a Maxwell-style fraud. What is more, unlike private sector workers, public sector employees do not run the risk of pension losses arising from the bankruptcy of their employer.

In 2002, the UK government signalled its intention to reform public sector pensions. The Green Paper 'Simplicity, Security and Choice: Working and Saving for Retirement' (DWP 2002) proposes a five-year increase in the retirement age for most public sector workers. While existing employees would be unaffected, new public servants would be required to work till age 65. Exceptions would be made for the police, fire-fighters and military personnel, since the physical fitness requirements of these jobs justify retirement at an earlier age. Individuals who leave these occupations before the normal age of retirement would not be able to take their pensions until they reached 65. Although 65 is currently the official retirement age for local government workers, their scheme rules permit individuals with sufficient years of service to retire at 60. The Green Paper proposes that this arrangement should be phased out.

Some countries have already reformed their public sector pensions. Until the early 1990s, Italian public servants were able to accrue entitlements to a full pension after just 20 years. Among other things, the Amato reform of 1992 (discussed more fully in Brugiavini and Fornero 2001, Forni and Giordano 2001) extended the contribution period to 35 years. Reforms were made to the Finnish public sector scheme, also in 1992, which raised the retirement age for public servants from 63 after 30 years service to 65 after 40 years. The replacement rate for public sector workers was also cut from 66 per cent to 60 per cent (Herbertsson *et al.*, 2000).

1.7 FINAL SALARY WOES

After more than a hundred years in operation, the future of salary-related occupational pension schemes is uncertain. It is likely that the retirement benefits they provide will in the future be much less generous than they were in the past. These schemes could even disappear altogether. They have become expensive to run; so expensive, in fact, that dozens of major employers have recently closed their final salary schemes to new employees, offering them cheaper money purchase schemes instead. A study of occupational pension scheme trends among 336 firms employing 1.8 million workers, undertaken by the Association of Consulting Actuaries (ACA 2002), found that 46 per cent of final salary schemes covered by the survey had been closed to new entrants. Some firms, the Big Food Group for example, have wound up their final salary schemes completely and offer DC schemes to existing as well as new employees.

Recent increases in the cost of final salary schemes are due to three main factors. These are the maturing of the schemes themselves, changes in their legal, fiscal and regulatory positions, and over-reliance by sponsors on equity investments. When they were first set up, employers' final salary schemes were cheap to run. It would typically take 40 years for workers to accrue entitlements to maximum pension benefits. Pension liabilities were therefore low, since those who retired in the first few years following a scheme's introduction were entitled to receive relatively small pensions. After several decades, though, liabilities had increased enormously, because large numbers of workers were approaching retirement age having built up entitlements to substantial pension pay-outs.

Although maturation is an inherent feature of final salary schemes, increases in life expectancy accelerated the process. Rising life expectancy meant that a growing number of workers were accruing pension entitlements right up to retirement age. It also meant that pensions had to be paid over a longer period. Until the late 1980s, employers had the legal right to make membership of their final salary schemes a condition of employment. In 1988, however, legislation came into force which outlawed compulsory membership of all occupational schemes. Whilst the legislation sought to give workers more choice in their pension arrangements – they could choose to contribute to SERPS, join a company scheme or pay into a personal pension plan – it had the effect of reducing the flow of contributions into final salary schemes. Currently, around a million employees choose not to join an occupational scheme, even though their employer provides one (Segars 2002). As a result, the economies of scale available to occupational schemes are lower than they would otherwise be, since the fixed costs of providing employees with pensions are being spread over fewer scheme members.

Since the 1920s, pension fund investments, like contributions, had been exempt from taxation. In 1997, though, the financing position of occupational schemes was worsened when the government withdrew their entitlement to receive dividend tax credits (DTCs). Until then, UK funded pension schemes had been able to reclaim the advance corporation tax paid on the dividend income they received from equity investments. In 1997, the value of DTCs to occupational pension schemes was around £5 billion a year. Their withdrawal meant that, for the first time in more than 50 years, different sources of pension fund income were taxed differently, because contributions, interest, rent and capital gains remain tax free. The implications of this for pension fund investment decisions is discussed further on in this section.

The withdrawal of DTCs reduced the returns earned on pension scheme investments. This raised the funding rate – the amount of money employers must contribute in order to keep DB schemes solvent. Thus, the scrapping of pension fund DTCs made it more expensive for employers to provide their workers with final salary pensions. To make matters worse, the scrapping of DTCs coincided with the introduction of legislation, passed in 1995, which imposed much stricter solvency requirements on final salary schemes and made benefit indexation compulsory. The implications of tighter solvency requirements are discussed more fully in Section 2.8. It is sufficient to note here that, prior to 1997, DB schemes were not necessarily deemed to be under-funded even where the market value of the assets they held was substantially less than their liabilities.

The introduction of compulsory indexation of occupational pensions – up to a maximum of 5 per cent per annum – is a major improvement for beneficiaries. Formerly, the indexation of pensions in payment was discretionary. This meant that pensioners could lose out to inflation which eroded the real value of benefits from those schemes which did not apply price indexation. With just 2 per cent inflation, for example, the real value of pension benefits which are not indexed to prices will be reduced by a third after 20 years. Compulsory indexation only applies to benefits accrued since 5 April 1997. Nevertheless, Davis (2001) notes that it has added an estimated £165 million a year to the cost of occupational schemes.

Because it reduced the returns that occupational schemes could earn on equity investments, the scrapping of DTCs made investing in bonds relatively more attractive. Even so, the vast majority of schemes remained heavily invested in equities. This left them extremely vulnerable to a collapse in share prices. The most vulnerable of all were mature final salary schemes with lots of short term liabilities. The 48 per cent fall in UK share values that occurred between September 2000 and February 2003 (Figure 1.7.1) created huge funding shortfalls for dozens of these schemes. Unless share values increase substantially over the next few years, the only way employers can honour their outstanding pension promises will be to inject large amounts of cash into their final salary schemes.

The pharmaceutical, cosmetics and personal care products retailer Boots plc was one British company which was not caught out by falling share prices. During the 18 months to July 2001, Boots's final salary scheme moved all its assets, 75 per cent of which had previously been invested in equities, into high-quality bonds. Although the company has never put the decision to get out of equities down to foresight, its timing could hardly have been better. The shares held by its final salary scheme were disposed of at an average FTSE 100 level of 6,000. By early 2003, the FTSE 100 – an index of the share values of 100 leading companies – had fallen below 3,700. The switch to bonds not only immunised the Boots scheme from the effects of falling equity values, it also preserved an

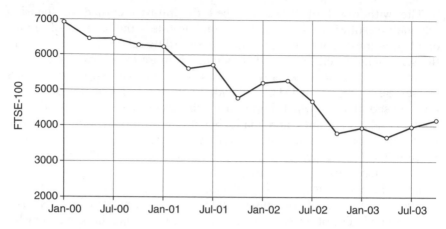

Figure 1.7.1 FTSE-100 levels, January 2000 to October 2003 (Datastream).

actuarial surplus at a time when other companies were having to cope with widening deficits.

Until it began selling off its shareholdings, the Boots scheme – with three-quarters of its assets invested in equities – was fairly typical of final salary schemes in the UK. This high level of equity exposure contrasted sharply with investment practices in the 1960s and 1970s, when equity investments accounted for a much smaller proportion of pension fund assets. The current vogue for very high levels of equity investment was triggered by the stockmarket boom of the 1980s. Sponsors quickly realised that rapidly rising equity returns could reduce the amounts they needed to pay into their pension schemes. Between 1979 and 1989, the proportion of pension fund investments allocated to domestic and foreign equities rose from 50 per cent to 66 per cent (Blake 1992). By the end of the 1990s, some companies had as much as 80 per cent of their pension scheme assets invested in shares.

The response of the trades unions and workers in general to the closing of dozens of final salary schemes and the winding up of others has, predictably perhaps, been one of outrage. Speaking on the eve of the 2003 conference of the Trades Union Congress (TUC), John Monks, normally regarded as a moderate TUC leader, declared himself to be a militant when it comes to pensions. Workers, he said, were being betrayed by employers and were now suffering a pensions crisis. The unions recognise that the funding problems faced by employers are not entirely of their own making. Indeed, union leaders were highly critical of the decision to scrap pension scheme DTCs. Nevertheless, the unions believe that, since employers have profited greatly from pension scheme surpluses in the past, they have a moral duty to make good today's shortfalls.

In the 1980s, most final salary schemes accumulated substantial financial surpluses. Some schemes built up surpluses which were considerably greater than the market value of their sponsoring firms. These surpluses arose for two reasons. First, large numbers of workers were leaving final salary schemes early, as firms sought to boost efficiency by shedding labour. This had the effect of slowing down the rate at which pension liabilities grew. Second, the value of pension scheme assets – an increasing proportion of which were being invested in equities – rose rapidly due to a booming stock market. For example, the value of assets held by UK pension schemes rose from around £40 billion at the end of 1979 to £150 billion at the end of 1985 (Griffiths 1986).

After concerns were expressed by the Inland Revenue about the tax losses implied by pension scheme surpluses, the government took action, in the second half of the 1980s, to limit the extent of over-funding. The 1986 Finance Act contained provisions which required sponsors with seriously over-funded schemes to bring their surpluses down to no more than 5 per cent of liabilities within five years. To comply with this requirement, firms with over-funded schemes could enhance pension benefits, suspend employer and/or employee contributions or have the surplus refunded (OPB 1997). Surplus refunds – known as asset reversions – were, however, subject to taxation at the rate of 40 per cent. Although increased pensions and suspended or reduced employee contributions would benefit scheme members, many sponsors chose to claw back part or all of their scheme surpluses via an employer's contribution holiday (Blake 1992).

Contributions holidays and asset reversions were not the only means available to sponsors who wished to capture pension scheme surpluses for their own use. By taking over another firm and transferring its employees to its own pension scheme, predator firms could strip out any surplus assets in the acquired company's scheme. Alternatively, firms could substitute a new scheme for an existing one. In both cases the members of one scheme, along with the assets necessary to back their accrued entitlements, would be transferred to another one. Because any surplus from the original scheme would revert to the sponsor, this method of capturing surpluses became known as 'spin-off termination'. As Davis (2001) observes, however, two judgements in the late 1980s relating to Hanson plc – discussed more fully in Blake (1992) – severely restricted the ability of firms to capture pension scheme surpluses via spin-off terminations.

Even though the issue currently facing many final salary schemes is one of under- rather than over-funding, surpluses are bound to re-emerge at some point in the future. For this not to happen, the rate of growth of final salary liabilities and the level of returns to pension scheme assets would have to match the assumptions that actuaries make about them on a permanent basis. In UK law, ownership of a pension scheme surplus is deemed to lie with the sponsoring employer. The logic for this is that since employers are obliged to make up any actuarial shortfalls that may emerge, they are also entitled to recover any surpluses that might arise. Because part of any surplus derives from the investment returns to contributions made by employees, though, it can be argued that sponsors should not have complete discretion over the use of these funds. Instead, they should be required to use the part of any surplus arising from moneys contributed by employees to enhance benefits or reduce workers' contributions.

1.8 INDIVIDUAL PENSIONS

Individual pension plans allow workers to save independently for their retirement. They are defined contribution arrangements which are provided by life insurance companies and other financial services providers, rather than by employers or governments. These plans differ from other savings vehicles in two important respects. First, contributors cannot normally withdraw their funds before they reach pensionable age. Second, withdrawal involves the annuitisation of most or all of the accumulated funds, to provide contributors with an income for the rest of their lives. As with many occupational and public schemes, individual plans often permit pensions to be drawn early on grounds of invalidity.

Though a relatively recent innovation in Britain, individual pension plans have been available in the United States since the mid-1970s. Individual Retirement Accounts (IRAs) were introduced in 1974, for employees who did not have access to a company pension scheme. They were subsequently made available to all workers and their families in 1981. Individual pensions for the self-employed have existed in the US since 1962. Participation in IRAs and the equivalent plans for the self-employed has, however, been at a fairly low level. In some Latin American countries, where participation is mandatory, take-up of individual pension plans is almost universal. Chile was the first Latin American country to introduce a system of compulsory individual saving for retirement, as an alternative to public pensions, in 1981. A number of other countries in the region quickly followed suit. By contrast, in Japan and much of Europe individual pension plans are virtually non-existent.

In the United Kingdom, individual plans are of two main types: personal pension plans and stakeholder pensions. Personal pension plans (PPPs) became available to all employees in mid-1988, although the enabling legislation was passed in 1986. Contributions to these plans are tax free and subject to an upper limit, and pensions may be taken at any time between the ages of 50 and 75. Although the funds accrued in PPPs must be used to purchase an annuity, up to 25 per cent may be taken as a tax-free lump sum. All workers who are not members of contracted-out occupational schemes are free to leave SERPS and have part of their National Insurance contributions diverted to a PPP of their choice. Before 1988, the option to save for retirement via an individual pension plan was only available to the self-employed. By 2001, the amount of money invested in individual pension plans stood at £345 billion, compared with just £50 billion in 1987 (Stears 2003).

Enthusiasm for PPPs was initially high, with take-up greatly exceeding official expectations (Disney and Whitehouse 1992). These plans were aggressively marketed, and to encourage take up the government was willing, for a limited period, to rebate 2 per cent of worker's past NICs into their PPPs. By the end of 1990, more than four and a half million people had left SERPs and taken out a PPP. The reputation of these plans was soon dented, however, when, in the early 1990s, it became apparent that more than a million workers had been wrongly advised to leave generous DB occupational schemes and take out less favourable PPPs. The process of identifying and compensating those affected took years to complete. In March 2002, for example, there were about 7,000 cases of mis-sold PPPs still awaiting settlement. The personal pensions mis-selling scandal is discussed in more detail in Section 2.10.

Through the introduction of PPPs, the government sought to achieve three objectives: to reduce the future cost of SERPs, to increase the take up of private pensions, and to promote greater labour market flexibility. In the early 1980s, the government was becoming increasingly alarmed by projections of rapidly rising expenditures on SERPS. Personal pensions could help to reduce the rate at which SERPS expenditures would grow. This is because by opting to have part of their NICs channelled into their personal pensions, contributors to PPPs – like members of contracted-out occupational schemes who pay reduced NICS – give up the SERPS benefits that their NI contributions would have bought. Emmerson and Johnson (2003) note that by the early 1990s, around three-quarters of those eligible to opt out of SERPS had actually done so. Around 50 per cent were members of occupational schemes, with the remaining 25 per cent contributing to PPPs.

With membership of occupational schemes stable at around 50 per cent of the employed workforce, there was considerable scope for extending participation in private pensions. Although membership of occupational schemes was high among public sector workers and employees of large private sector companies, within some sections of the workforce rates of participation were particularly low (Disney and Whitehouse 1992). Membership of occupational schemes was usually denied to part-time workers. This meant that large numbers of women had no access to a private pension, since females dominated this large and growing segment of the workforce (Sullivan 1996b). At the same time, many small firms, especially those in the service sector, did not provide their employees with occupational pensions. PPPs would allow part-timers and employees of small firms to contribute to their own private pensions, because the option to take out a personal pension was not restricted to any particular category of worker.

PPPs would also be fully portable. Unlike members of DB occupational schemes, contributors to PPPS would not suffer a financial penalty if they changed employers. Thus PPPs would help to make the labour market more flexible by permitting workers to change jobs more easily. Whilst it was never the intention that occupational scheme members should leave their schemes and take out a PPP, there seems to have been an expectation that, given the choice, new entrants to the labour market would opt for a personal pension. For this reason, the 1986 Social Security Act, which established the legal basis for the provision of PPPs, also abolished the right of employers to compel workers to join their company pension schemes.

In seeking to use privately provided individual pensions to reduce future public pension expenditures, the British government had drawn inspiration from the Chilean pension reform of November 1980. The Chilean reform, which took effect in 1981, was part of a wider process of privatisation begun in the 1970s, following the overthrow of president Salvador Allende in a military coup lead by General Augusto Pinochet. The purpose of the reform was twofold: to save Chile's PAYG social security system from bankruptcy and to increase the level of domestic saving in order to reduce foreign borrowing and create a system of capital markets (Mittelstaedt 2003). At the time, Chile's corporate sector held large amounts of foreign debt, having previously engaged in heavy borrowing from abroad to finance the acquisition of businesses which had formerly been nationalised by the Socialist government of President Allende.

Instead of making public pension contributions, since 1981 Chilean workers have been compelled to pay 10 per cent of their monthly earnings into personal DC plans known as individual capitalisation accounts. To provide these plans, special private sector organisations known as AFPs (Asociaciones de Fondos de Pensiones) were set up. AFPs charge planholders a commission – which comprises a flat fee plus a percentage of the salary used to determine contributions – to cover their administration costs and the cost of providing life and disability insurance. Competition between AFPs is intended to ensure that commissions are kept low. There are no switching costs, so although workers cannot have accounts with more than one AFP, they can change AFPs more or less at will. Workers' contributions to their capitalisation accounts, and the investment returns earned, are tax free, and their accumulated funds must be used to purchase an indexed annuity at retirement. A degree of income drawdown is also possible. For a discussion of indexed annuities and income drawdown, see Section 2.5.

The 1980 reform did not take the Chilean government out of pension provision altogether. Instead of collecting contributions and paying pensions, though, its activities are now mainly confined to the supervision of AFPs and the provision of an income safety-net for pensioners. As well as providing for the destitute old, if workers with 20 years of contributions retire with insufficient funds in their capitalisation accounts to provide them with a minimum pension income, the government guarantees to make up the difference. Should an AFP fail, its investors' funds are protected by a 100 per cent government guarantee. Such guarantees can, however, induce fund managers to take excessive risks with their clients' funds – an issue which is discussed at greater length in Section 2.9. To safeguard against excessive risk-taking, AFPs are subject to regulations governing, among other things, their investment practices, the rates of return they deliver and the information they provide to customers.

Whilst Chile was the first country to compel its citizens to save for their old age with private pension companies, it was not the first to introduce compulsory individual retirement saving. A system of individual saving for retirement has operated in Singapore since 1955 (Davis 1995, Chia and Tsui 2003). In Singapore, however, workers' pension savings are collected and invested by state-run agencies. The system is administered by the Central Provident Fund (CPF), with the Government of Singapore Investment Corporation and the Monetary Authority of Singapore managing the investment of workers' accumulated funds. At retirement, workers must use their funds to purchase a life annuity providing an income equal to 25 per cent of average earnings. Any remaining moneys may be withdrawn as a lump sum.

As in Chile, the Singapore government provides a basic pension income for individuals with no retirement savings. It also guarantees a minimum replacement rate for those whose retirement savings are small. Unlike Chilean AFPs, the CPF does not incur marketing costs because it doesn't have to compete for savers' funds. This, combined with the scale economies arising from its having a monopoly on pension savings, means that operating costs are low – 0.5 per cent of contributions in the 1990s (Davis 1995). In Britain, where PPPs are privately administered, relatively high operating costs and the need for providers to make a profit means that personal pensions are a rather expensive form of individual saving for retirement.

The charges levied by UK PPP providers are equivalent to a reduction in contributions of between 10 and 20 percent over the life of these plans (Blake 2000). They are prohibitively expensive, therefore, for workers with modest incomes. What is more, PPPs have rigid contribution schedules. The requirement for contributions to be made on a regular basis means that they are only suitable for those in continuous employment. Thus, a combination of high charges and rigid contribution schedules effectively prevents large numbers of part-time and temporary workers who have low or irregular earnings from taking out a PPP. PPPs are also unavailable to children and adults who are not currently in employment.

In April 2001, stakeholder pensions were introduced as a low-cost and flexible alternative to PPPs. As with PPPs, contributions and investment returns are tax free, and at least 75 per cent of the terminal fund must be annuitised between the ages of 50 and 75. While these plans are available to anyone, they were primarily aimed at the seven million or so workers who, in 2001, were not making any form of private pension contributions. Unlike PPPs, contributions to stakeholder plans can be made through high-street outlets such as banks, supermarkets and post offices. Providers' charges are lower than for PPPs, being capped at 1 per cent of the annual value of a contributor's accumulated fund. Individual contributions can be as low as £20, with plan-holders free to choose when contributions are made.

As Table 1.8.1 shows, within a year of their launch, more than three-quarters of a million people had taken up a stakeholder pension. It is unclear, however, how much additional pension saving this represented and how much was replacing contributions that would in any case have gone to other pension plans. Whilst caution needs to be exercised in interpreting the figures in the table, it appears that 90 per cent of stakeholder pensions taken up by or for people of working age were receiving regular contributions, rather than one-off payments up to the maximum of £3,600. The average amount contributed was £972 per annum – £81 per month. Moreover, more than 300,000 were taken up by low- to middle-income earners – individuals with incomes between £10,000 and £20,000 per year – the kind of workers the government was most keen to see take them up. Only 2 per cent of the 750,000 stakeholder pensions taken up were for children, and 1 per cent for people over 65. Of employers, 320,000 had designated a stakeholder provider for their employees, as the law requires.

Although contributors to individual pension plans do not experience portability losses in the way that members of DB occupational schemes can do when they change employers, they are exposed to other risks. A variety of problems can arise during the accumulation phase – when contributions are being paid. The returns earned on invested contributions may be less than expected, with the result that terminal funds turn out to be lower than originally anticipated. In addition, contributors may

Table 1.8.1 Number of stakeholder contracts sold in first year of operation, by category of purchaser

Purchaser	Contracts sold in first year
Children	15,000
Aged 65+	7,000
Working age with no earnings	57,000
Working age earning less than £10,000	117,500
Working age earning £10,000–£19,999	319,500
Working age earning £20,000–£29,999	130,000
Working age earning £30,000+	106,500
Total	752,000

Source: Grainge *et al.* (2002).

experience difficulty maintaining contributions – due, for example, to loss of employment – such that their plans either grow more slowly than expected or lapse altogether. There is also the risk that the value of terminal funds will be reduced by an untimely fall in asset values, forcing people to postpone retirement or to accept a smaller annuity than they had hoped for. Finally, the value of retirement benefits that can be bought with plan-holders' terminal funds may be reduced by a fall in annuity rates, which vary in line with changes in bond interest rates. The main risk arising during the decumulation phase – when pensions are being paid – is the insolvency of the annuity provider.

1.9 PENSIONERS' INCOMES

It was noted in Section 1.1 that pensions are just one of a number of sources of income available to retired people. Pensions cannot properly be understood, therefore, without an appreciation of the contribution they make to pensioners' total retirement incomes. In some countries, Greece and Italy for example, virtually all the income received by retired people comes from public pension payments. In others – such as the US and the UK – the composition of post-retirement incomes is more diverse. A detailed international comparison of pensioners' incomes is beyond the scope of this book; see instead Disney and Whitehouse (2001). The focus here is on the level, structure and distribution of post-retirement incomes in Britain.

The history of pension provision in Britain is one of continuous evolution. Since 1979, however, the pace of change has been particularly rapid. New types of private pension scheme have been established, and the rules governing the operation of existing schemes have been changed many times. The way entitlements to a pension from SERPs are calculated and the method of uprating the BSP have also been changed. New means-tested benefits for the elderly have been introduced, along with alterations to the way in which entitlements to existing benefits are assessed. At the same time, pensioners' incomes have risen rapidly. Between the calendar year 1979 and the financial year 1996–1997, the real incomes of retired people grew almost twice as fast as those of the population as a whole. Together, these changes, along with changes in labour market conditions, have had and will continue to have a major influence upon the level, composition and distribution of pensioner incomes.

In most industrialised countries, the incomes of pensioners are treated more favourably by the tax system than the incomes of non-pensioners. Indeed, in many countries tax concessions for retirees are an important element of the state's overall financial commitment to the elderly (Keenay and Whitehouse 2003). In Britain, the income threshold at which tax becomes payable is higher for individuals over state pension age than it is for younger people – £6,610 per annum, compared with £4,615, in 2003–2004. In addition, NICs are not payable on pension incomes, even where recipients are under state pension age. Consequently, the direct tax burden borne by pensioners is lighter than that borne by individuals of working age.

In the financial year 2001–2002, the average income of all pensioner units – single pensioners and couples where the man is retired – was estimated by the Department for Work and Pensions at £229 per week. Analysis of the data on pensioner incomes, however, reveals substantial differences in economic circumstances within and between different groups of retired people. Single men typically have higher incomes than women. Older pensioners of both sexes tend to have lower incomes than their younger counterparts, and younger pensioners have benefited the most from the recent growth in post-retirement incomes. While many pensioners are currently enjoying a relatively high standard of living, more than a third have sufficiently low incomes to qualify for a variety of means-tested social security benefits.

Estimates of the distribution of pensioner incomes in 2001–2002, before and after housing costs are taken into account, are presented in Table 1.9.1. Housing costs include: rent and mortgage interest payments net of tax relief, ground rent and service charges, structural insurance premiums, water rates and council water charges. The table shows that, before housing costs, the most affluent pensioner couples had incomes more than three and a quarter times greater than those received by the least well-off couples. After housing costs are accounted for, the difference was more than three and a half times greater. Similar differences can be observed in the incomes received by single pensioners.

Table 1.9.2 shows estimates for the average incomes of pensioner couples and individual pensioners, before and after housing costs. It can be seen that single women on average received £29 per week less than single men, and £7 per week less than all lone pensioners, before housing

Table 1.9.1 Estimated median net income of pensioner units (£ per week) by quintile of the net income distribution, 2001–2002

	Bottom fifth	Next fifth	Middle fifth	Next fifth	Top fifth
Before housing costs					
Pensioner couples	155	203	251	329	510
Single pensioners	87	120	148	182	261
After housing costs					
Pensioner couples	136	183	236	313	498
Single pensioners	71	94	118	161	238

Source: DWP (2003).

Table 1.9.2 Estimated average net income (£ per week) of pensioner units, 2001–2002

	Pensioner couples	Single pensioners	Men	Women
Before housing costs	322	167	189	160
After housing costs	303	143	165	135

Source: DWP (2003).

costs. Once housing costs are taken into account, the gap between male and female incomes widens to £30 per week. Consequently, the retirement incomes of single women were 84.7 per cent of male incomes before housing costs, but only 81.8 per cent after housing costs.

Gender differences in the post-retirement incomes of single pensioners reflect the fact that the UK's pension arrangements have been, and continue to be, less favourable for women than men. Until 1978, state pension arrangements were largely based on the presumption that married women were economic dependants of their husbands and should not be expected to contribute to a pension in their own right. Whereas single women were required to pay full NICs, married women in employment could opt to contribute at a lower married women's rate (MWR), which did not entitle them to a pension when they reached retirement age. This arrangement has proven to be especially problematic for divorced women, who, following their divorce, often had insufficient working years left to build up entitlement to a full pension. Although the option to pay NICS at the MWR was withdrawn in 1978, those already doing so were permitted to continue contributing at the lower rate.

Private pension schemes have proven to be equally disadvantageous for women. As Section 1.5 shows, female employees have always had lower rates of participation in occupational schemes than male workers. Thus, although many widows receive survivors' benefits from their husband's schemes, far fewer women than men enter retirement with an occupational pension of their own. Furthermore, women who do have their own occupational pensions typically receive lower benefits than men. This is because occupational schemes – whether defined benefit or defined contribution – work best for those with uninterrupted employment patterns and the highest earnings. They tend to be less favourable for women, who, on average, have lower earnings than men and who, for family reasons, are more likely to take time out of formal employment.

Table 1.9.3 highlights the differences in the incomes of younger and older pensioners. It can be seen that, in 2001–2002, before housing costs are accounted for, the incomes of pensioner couples aged under 75 were some 26 per cent greater than those of couples aged 75 and over. The difference after housing costs was 28 per cent. Single pensioners under 75

Table 1.9.3 Estimated average net income (£ per week) of pensioner units by age,
2001–2002

	Pensioner couples	Single pensioners
Under 75		
Before housing costs	347	175
After housing costs	328	150
75 and over		
Before housing costs	275	160
After housing costs	256	137

Source: DWP (2003).

had incomes 9.4 per cent greater than those aged 75 and over, before
housing costs, and 9.5 percent greater after. Although, as Figure 1.9.1
shows, 60 per cent of all pensioner units had some income from occupational pensions, and nearly 70 per cent had some income from investments, state pension and other benefit payments represented a larger
proportion of the total incomes of couples aged 75 and over, compared
with younger couples.

Age differences in the incomes of single pensioners also reflect disparities in the proportions of total incomes derived from different sources. As
Table 1.9.4 shows, on average, newly retired people – men aged between
65 and 70 and women between 60 and 65 – derived half of their total
incomes from state pensions and other benefit payments in 2001–2002.
This compares with 59 per cent for all single pensioners under 75 and 66
per cent for those aged 75 and over. The fact that women represent nearly
two-thirds of all single pensioners aged 75 and over is another important
explanatory factor in this group's lower retirement incomes. Not only do
these women typically receive less than their younger counterparts from
occupational pensions and investments; they also benefited less from the
introduction, in 1978, of home responsibilities protection (HRP). HRP fills
in NIC contributions gaps by providing National Insurance credits for
workers who take time out of employment to raise children or care for
sick relatives.

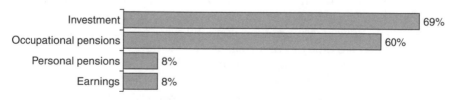

Figure 1.9.1 Proportion of all pensioners with some non-state pension income, by
source, 2001–2002 (DWP (2003)).

Table 1.9.4 Estimated percentages of average single pensioner incomes by age and source, 2001–2002

	Recently retired	*Under 75*	*75 and over*
State pensions and other benefits	51	59	66
Occupational pensions	21	24	22
Investments including personal pensions	2	1	1
Earnings	16	8	1
Other	2	1	1

Source: DWP (2003).

Eliminating pension poverty has been a high-profile government objective in the UK since the election of the first Blair administration, in 1997. To achieve this objective, the government has granted a number of ad hoc above inflation increases in the BSP and increased the generosity of pensioners' means-tested benefits. These increases in pension payments and means-tested benefits have resulted in a reduction in the percentage of all pensioners with incomes below 60 per cent of the median income – the government's main measure of pensioner poverty. As Table 1.9.5 shows, between 1996 and 2002, the proportion of pensioners with incomes below 60 per cent of the median income after taking account of housing costs fell from 27 per cent to 22 per cent.

Table 1.9.5 Percentage of pensioners with incomes below 60 per cent of the median income, 1996–2002

	1996–1997	*1997–1998*	*1998–1999*	*1999–2000*	*2000–2001*	*2001–2002*
Before housing costs	21	22	23	22	21	22
After housing costs	27	27	27	25	24	22

Source: Goodman *et al.* (2003).

Part 2

Pensions

Issues and controversies

2.1 POPULATION AGEING IN PERSPECTIVE

Population ageing is a hot topic. Over the past two decades, thousands of academic papers have been written on the subject. National and international bodies have researched the issue, publishing their findings in often voluminous reports. Population ageing is the subject of a growing number of conferences, books, TV and radio programmes, and is the theme of innumerable articles and press reports. The title of one of the most well-known publications on the subject, *Averting The Old Age Crisis*, (World Bank 1994) aptly illustrates the approach to population ageing most commonly adopted. Population ageing is an inexorable process which, in the absence of immediate and far-reaching reforms, amounts to a demographic time bomb that will eventually blow apart the public pension and healthcare systems of many developed and developing countries. For some – Peterson (1999), for example – the prospect of older populations implies a future characterised by social ossification and intergenerational conflict, with a relatively small number of young, productive people competing with a much larger group of old, unproductive individuals for a finite supply of economic resources.

The age bomb scenario is especially alarming because it has about it an air of common sense and inevitability. Population ageing is a potential disaster which is already unfolding. The people who, 30 or 40 years from now, will be aged 65 and over are already alive, and there's an awful lot of them. What's more, we're having too few children to maintain the existing population balance between the young and the old. The inescapable conclusion, then, is that the ratio of old, inactive and dependent people to younger, active and productive individuals will worsen significantly over the coming decades. Healthcare and pension costs will spiral, and the tax burden on working-age people will become intolerable. The reality of population ageing may, however, turn out to be rather different. Current projections of population ageing may ultimately prove to have been excessively pessimistic. Even if they turn out to be correct, the economic, social and political impact may be far less severe than the demographic doomsters predict.

The size and age distribution of a future population will be determined by past events and by events which are yet to happen. It is not possible, therefore, to say with certainty what a population will look like 40 or 50 years hence. While past trends in births, deaths and migratory flows are knowable, demographers can only make assumptions about the future paths these variables will take. Consequently, population projections are not predictions of what a future population will actually look like. They are, instead, extrapolations, forecasts of what it would look like if the assumptions on which they are based turn out to be true. Thus, projections of a much older population in the future are descriptions of a possibility, which has some degree of probability but is not a certainty. Moreover, as

Hinde (1998) shows, the more distant the projections, the greater the degree of uncertainty they will possess.

The population projections for the UK shown in Part 1 assume that life expectancy will continue to rise, albeit at a diminishing rate. They also assume that fertility will remain low. The first of these assumptions seems fairly probable, given the pace of developments in medicine and the care of the elderly. The second looks much less certain. Fertility is largely a matter of choice. What is more, choices about the number of children to have are not taken in isolation. They are influenced by the prevailing social, economic and cultural environment. Because women are currently choosing to have relatively few children does not mean they will always do so.

Recent changes in the pattern of family formation suggest that fertility may, in the future, be somewhat higher than it is at present. Rather than having their children young, as in the late 1960s and 1970s, women have been postponing family formation, preferring instead to spend time acquiring qualifications and establishing themselves in careers during their early child-bearing years. Increasingly, women have been waiting until they are well over 30 before starting a family. In 1991 more than 26 per cent of first births were to women aged 30 and over, up from 15 per cent a decade earlier (Jackson 1998). Currently, 7 per cent of all births in the UK are to women aged 35 or more.

The tendency for women to delay starting a family has been accompanied by a trend among mothers for shorter intervals between the birth of their first child and that of any subsequent children. The trend is particularly marked, however, among women who start their families late. It seems, then, that those who delay starting a family are also choosing to complete their reproductive activity in fewer years than has historically been the norm. Such behaviour is perfectly rational, given that the probability of conception declines with age just as the likelihood of complications in pregnancy and the risk of producing children with birth abnormalities both increase. What it suggests, though, is that fertility may not be as low as the official estimates imply.

Around 30 per cent of British women in their mid-thirties have not yet had a child. It is impossible to know in advance how many of these women have chosen to postpone rather than forego family formation. Despite the risks, it makes sense for women to delay starting a family until they are better able to absorb the economic costs associated with child-rearing. What is more, advances in reproductive technology, obstetrics and genetics are extending the age limit for conception and reducing many of the traditional risks associated with childbirth at older ages. Many of today's childless thirty-somethings may go on to start families in their forties. Some may go on having children well into their fifties. Against this background, current fertility rates will tend to understate the real level of fecundity over the medium term. Consequently, projections of rising ratios of old to working age people based on today's low fertility rates may prove to be excessively pessimistic.

It would, of course, take around two decades before an upturn in fertility began to add to the working population. A more immediate way to boost the workforce would be through increased immigration. Immigrants are typically young. They also tend to be industrious and prepared to do jobs that indigenous workers spurn. Thus, immigration can swell a country's workforce and reduce general as well as sector-specific labour shortages. Immigration can also help to increase fertility, because newly arrived migrants tend to have higher rates of reproduction than the established population. Even if sufficient numbers of foreigners wished to live and work in Britain, though, it is unlikely that immigration alone could reverse population ageing. As Wallace (2001) points out, for this to happen the number of people permanently settling in the UK each year would have to rise to politically unsustainable levels. Nevertheless, even moderate levels of immigration can go some way towards reducing the rate at which the old age dependency ratio rises.

In the late 1990s, concerns about emerging skills shortages led the government to ease the restrictions on entry into Britain by non-EU citizens. A fast-track work permit scheme was established to allow employers in sectors with acute labour shortages to recruit more foreign workers. In 2002, schools and hospitals were reported to be recruiting large numbers of workers from overseas. Faced with thousands of unfilled vacancies, the Metropolitan Police recently announced that it was also considering recruiting officers from abroad. Like the migrant workers who, each summer, pick, wash and pack vegetables on the farms of south-east England before returning home after the harvest, foreign teachers, nurses and other professionals are usually recruited on a temporary basis. Whilst there is an expectation that these workers will eventually return to their home countries, many may end up settling in Britain permanently. Although attitudes to immigration appear to be hardening at present – a response, in part, to unprecedented numbers of asylum seekers – economic necessity may engender a more welcoming approach in the future.

Projections of a demographic disaster have proved wrong in the past. In the 1920s and 1930s, the UK's fertility rate gradually declined, falling well below the 2.1 children per woman required to maintain a constant population size. Official concern about the implications of low fertility for the British economy was such that a Royal Commission on population was set up in 1944 to consider the problem (Jackson 1998). In its report, published in 1949, the Commission's findings made uncomfortable reading. On the assumption that fertility would remain low, the Commission forecast that the population would eventually begin to shrink. As the population contracted, it would also age rapidly. A shortage of young workers would emerge, undermining Britain's prospects for economic growth and development. Moreover, population ageing would result in a relatively small workforce struggling to meet a spiralling pensions bill. In the event, the baby boom of the 1950s and 1960s put an end to these fears.

Over the next half-century the ratio of elderly people to those of working age will certainly increase. The extent of the increase, however, cannot accurately be predicted. Although a baby boom on the scale of the one that occurred in the 1950s and 1960s is unlikely, there is no reason to suppose that today's low fertility rates will persist indefinitely. Governments could introduce policies to promote family formation. They may also adopt a more positive approach to immigration. Together, a modest increase in fertility combined with a more liberal approach to immigration would result in a lower than projected increase in the old age dependency ratio. Moreover, population ageing may itself turn out to be a more benign process than the prophets of demographic doom suggest.

In order to assess the true significance of population ageing it is necessary to look beyond the arithmetic of the old age dependency ratio. This is because, by themselves, changes in the ratio of old to working-age people only provide a simplified, one-dimensional, description of what is, in reality, a complex and multi-dimensional process. The old age dependency ratio is a statistical concept which utilises a purely chronological definition of old age. It assumes that people become old and dependent, rather than young and productive, as soon as they reach a particular age, usually 65. Yet ageing is a biological as well as a chronological phenomenon. Because the biological dimension to ageing is ignored, changes in the old age dependency ratio give an incomplete and arguably misleading picture of population ageing.

In biological terms, ageing is a process of physiological and intellectual decline which results from a gradual accumulation of damage to the cells and tissues of the body. Whilst some of this damage is due to external factors, much of it is self-inflicted. The ultraviolet radiation in sunlight damages human skin. Chemicals and other damaging agents in the environment are absorbed into the body. Overwork, a sedentary lifestyle and a fatty diet all help to break the body down. Tobacco smoke and alcohol wreak havoc on the lungs, the heart and the liver. The human body also attacks itself. Powerful oxidising agents known as free radicals – produced deep within the body's cells – constantly destroy chunks of DNA, the genetic material that governs the way in which cells reproduce themselves. Although the body is very efficient at repairing itself, some damage is irreparable. Human beings age as the volume of irreparable damage builds up over time.

Whereas people age chronologically at a constant rate – growing older by one year every year – the path of biological ageing exhibits no such regularity. The pace at which people's physical and mental capacities decline over time varies between individuals. Some people age faster than others in biological terms. The pace of biological ageing also varies between entire populations. Variations in the rate at which people age biologically reflect, among other things, differences in lifestyle, dietary habits and exposure to environmental hazards. The process of biological ageing is, then, a malleable phenomenon. Medical intervention, dietary improvements, taking exercise and a cleaner, safer environment can all reduce the rate at which biological ageing occurs.

Because the rate at which biological ageing proceeds can be reduced, people can grow old in the chronological sense long before they become biologically old. Moreover, medical advances and lifestyle improvements have the potential to permit successive generations to widen the gap between chronological and biological old age. Mullan (2000) presents evidence from a number of recent studies which suggests that, on average, today's over-65s are indeed experiencing fewer of the biological symptoms of old age than their predecessors. Today, people appear to be reaching the age of 65 in better shape, and maintaining good health for longer, than they did in the past. As Professor Tom Kirkwood put it in the first of his 2001 BBC Reith Lectures on ageing, "in many respects today's 70 year olds are like the 60 year olds of a generation or two ago". Thus, increases in the average age of the population, and increases in the proportion of people defined as old in chronological terms, cannot necessarily be taken to imply that society is becoming biologically older.

Improvements in the health of the elderly support the 'compression of morbidity' thesis put forward by James Fries in the 1980s (Fries 1980, 1988, 1989). The compression of morbidity thesis states that, as medical and other advances extend the healthy and active portion of the human lifespan, with life expectancy held constant the morbid period – the period between the onset of chronic ill health and death – will be squeezed into a shorter interval. Life will increasingly come to be characterised by a long period of health and vitality, followed by a rapid descent into illness and physical dependency just prior to death. The compression of morbidity will therefore allow the elderly population to grow in number without an equivalent increase in the burden of physical dependency. While increases in longevity have the potential to wipe out the gains from morbidity compression, Mullan (2000) presents evidence which suggests that the pace of improvements in the health of the elderly has recently been greater than the rate of increase in life expectancy.

The popularity of the demographic time-bomb scenario can be explained in terms of its strong psychological appeal. Images of a future society dominated by old people, where youth is a scarce commodity, pander to some of the most deeply rooted human fears and prejudices concerning the ageing process and the experience of being old. The perception of ageing, at least according to Western notions, is one of a gradual but accelerating transition, as the years go by, from a state of vigour and independence to one of decrepitude and dependency. Individuals pass from a condition of adaptability and openness to new ideas to one of increasing conservatism and resistance to change. To be old is to be 'past it', 'over the hill', 'finished', with only death to look forward to. Not a state to which most people would freely aspire.

The popular stereotype of elderly people as economically inactive dependants of the working population has, in fact, never been a very accurate depiction of what it means to be old. The compression of morbidity thesis suggests that it will become even less realistic in the future. Whilst the over-65s receive healthcare and pensions paid for by the working population, they also make a substantial economic contribution of their own. Many older people choose to remain in paid employment long after reaching state pension age. As work becomes less physically demanding and the level of fitness among older age groups rises, it is likely that even more people will elect to undertake paid work beyond retirement age. By working past retirement age older people can enjoy the social interaction that the workplace affords as well as earning an additional income. They can also bring to the workplace valuable skills and experience acquired over many decades. The charitable sector depends heavily upon the efforts of the elderly, because retired people do an enormous amount of unpaid voluntary work.

Even when older people are not directly employed, they may still be performing a valuable economic function. Because it is often indirect and hence invisible, though, much of the economic contribution made by the elderly often goes unrecognised. By transporting grandchildren to and from school or shopping for their children, they make it possible for younger people – particularly women – who would otherwise have to remain at home to enter the workplace. Elderly relatives are often on hand to look after a sick child or wait in for a delivery, tasks that would otherwise require a working parent to take time off. By baby-sitting their grandchildren, older people free their children to enjoy an evening out at the pub, the cinema, a restaurant and such like, thereby helping to create employment opportunities in the leisure industry.

Consumption of goods and services by elderly people themselves generates an enormous amount of economic activity. The concept of retirement as a time to sit back and do nothing very much – the reward for a busy working life – does not match the experience of growing numbers of retired people. As the number of people reaching retirement age with comfortable incomes and their health intact has risen, retirement has come to be regarded by many as the time to do the things they did not have the opportunity to do during their working lives. Companies like Saga have been established to supply travel and leisure services to the elderly. Garden centres, bingo halls and specialist hobby shops are all heavily patronised by older people. Participation by retired people in a wide range of educational courses generates employment for teachers and lecturers. Publicly and privately run homes providing residential care for the elderly infirm employ thousands of workers. In fact, output and employment in most sectors of the economy are, to a greater or lesser extent, dependent upon the consumption expenditure of pensioners. Moreover, the pensions industry is itself a major source of wealth creation and employment.

It was noted in Part 1 that successive British governments have introduced policies to limit the rate at which pension expenditures will rise as the population ages. The compression of morbidity thesis suggests that the associated increase in the health costs of the elderly may also be manageable. The projected increase in the ratio of pensioners to workers looks all the more affordable, viewed in the context of earnings growth. Over time, earned incomes rise as productivity increases. In the two and a half decades to 2000, real earnings grew by around 2 per cent per annum. If this trend continues, average earnings will have doubled between 2000 and 2035 and risen by a further 69 per cent by 2050. Rising incomes mean rising tax receipts. Thus, earnings growth permits higher spending on the elderly without the need to increase tax rates.

Baker and Weisbrot (1999) argue that in the coming decades wage rates are likely to be bid up, as employers compete for a dwindling supply of young workers; a consequence of low fertility today. In this case, earnings growth would exceed 2 per cent. If real earnings were to grow by an average of 3 per cent a year, earned incomes would have doubled by 2025 and more than tripled by 2050. Even if the rate of earnings growth turns out to be lower, at just 1.5 per cent per annum, earned incomes will still be 56 per cent higher in real terms in 2030 than they were in 2000. By 2050 they will be 111 per cent higher.

In addition to rising earnings, changes in the distribution of public expenditures will help to mitigate the financial impact of population ageing. As Table 2.1.1 shows, while the old age dependency ratio is projected to rise in the coming decades, the youth dependency ratio – the ratio of children under 16 to people of working age – is forecast to fall. Reductions in the youth dependency ratio will partially offset increases in the old age dependency ratio. Consequently, whereas the old age dependency ratio is projected to increase by 41.5 per cent between 2001 and 2051, the total dependency ratio – the ratio of children and pensioners to the working population – is forecast to rise by less than 14 per cent. A falling youth dependency ratio implies that tax-financed expenditures on education and health care for the young will also fall. Thus, the reduction in public expenditures on the young will, to some extent, compensate for higher spending on the elderly.

Table 2.1.1 Projected youth and total dependency ratios, 2001–2051

	2001	2011	2021	2031	2041	2051
Youth dependency ratio	0.33	0.29	0.28	0.29	0.29	0.29
Total dependency ratio	0.62	0.60	0.59	0.67	0.71	0.70

Source: Dunnell (2000).

2.2 LIVING AND WORKING FOR LONGER

Retirement is a comparatively modern invention. It is largely the product of industrialisation. As Sass (1997) points out, in the pre-industrial age the infirmities associated with old age did not rob individuals of their economic value. When production was small-scale and handicraft-based, the skills and experience people acquired in their youth helped to compensate for their diminished physical vitality in later life. Consequently, the old were expected to work – and usually did – unless sickness or disability prevented them from doing so. Since production was generally organised around familial units, the business of getting a living was a collective activity, with the relevant tasks being allocated among family members according to their individual capacities.

Industrialisation, however, changed both the scale and the pace of production. With mechanisation and the organisation of production on a large scale, earning a living became an individual activity. A person's labour became a commodity to be bought and sold in the market. Workers were needed who could toil for long hours, often at a machine's pace. Thus, physical strength and stamina became the main determinants of most people's economic value. As employees' physical powers, and hence their economic value, declined with age, their employers needed, in the interests of efficiency, to replace them with younger, fitter workers. By making it possible for aged employees to retire, through the provision of a pension, employers could maintain the efficiency of their organisations without having to dismiss these workers into penury.

As noted in Section 1.5, employer-provided pensions only became available to a small proportion of the workforce – mainly the employees of large organisations. Smaller employers were either unwilling or unable to bear the cost of supporting their former employees financially. With no alternative means of support, most workers laboured on into old age for as long as their employers were prepared to keep them. It was not until the arrival of public pensions that retirement in the form of a permanent and voluntary withdrawal from employment became a genuine possibility for the mass of the working population.

Even before public pensions were introduced, politicians worried about their cost to the taxpayer. Although public schemes were set up to provide financial assistance for those who were too old to derive an income from employment and who had no alternative means of support, the choice of retirement age was made principally on the basis of cost. As Thane (1978) notes, in Britain it was generally agreed that 65 was the age at which most people's physical powers had declined to the point where they were no longer capable of regular work. Yet, as in Germany – the first country to set up a public pension scheme, in 1889 – 70 was chosen as the official retirement age for the British scheme, established nearly two decades later.

In fact, as Section 1.2 notes, Britain's 1908 scheme was hardly a pension scheme at all. Rather, it was a mechanism for delivering poor relief to the destitute old. The insurance principle was not introduced until 1925, when the Widows', Orphans' and Old Age Contributory Pensions Act was passed. The 1925 Act also reduced the retirement age by 5 years to 65. Change came again when, in 1940, the retirement age for women was reduced to 60. The justification for a lower female retirement age appears to have been the average five-year age gap, at that time, between married couples. With men, on average, five years older than their wives, the change made it possible for the typical couple to enter retirement together. Further change is set to occur from 2010, when the age of retirement for women will rise – over a 10-year period – to equal that of men once more.

The Green Paper (DWP 2002) makes it clear that beyond the planned five-year increase in the female retirement age the present government does not propose to compel people to work for longer. Instead, it intends to strengthen the incentives that already exist for people to work past the age of 65 voluntarily and to introduce new ones. In addition, legislation outlawing age discrimination in the workplace planned for 2006 is to be brought forward and the right of employers to specify retirement ages in contracts of employment is to be abolished. Although a case for a mandatory increase in the state pension age can be made, there are good reasons for thinking that persuading rather than compelling people to work for longer is the right approach.

The case for raising the state pension age to perhaps 68 or 70 is straightforward. Average life expectancy is now more than 10 years longer than it was when the state pension age was first set at 65 for both men and women. Furthermore, improvements in the health of older people mean that 65 is no longer the age at which the average person's physical and mental powers have declined to the point where they are unable to work in order to support themselves. Raising the state pension age by a few years would not be especially burdensome for today's workers. It would simply be a logical response to changed circumstances.

A moderate increase in the state pension age would have a number of beneficial effects on Britain's public pension finances. First, pension costs would be reduced, because some workers who would have retired at 65, but died soon after, would never reach the higher retirement age. Second, because the period during which individuals received retirement benefits would be shorter, total pension payments for each individual would be lower – assuming no compensating actuarial benefit adjustment. Finally, more money would be available to pay pensions, since people would make contributions beyond the age of 65. Unfortunately, though, the impact of an increase in the state pension age would bear more heavily on some individuals than it would on others.

Although people live longer today, and are healthier than ever before, disparities can be observed in the health and mortality experience of different socio-economic groups. In Britain and the United States, individuals' life expectancies and health status have been shown to vary substantially, according to their gender, ethnicity and income levels (Victor 1991, Baker and Weisbrot 1999, Weller 2000, Attanasio and Emmerson 2001). Consequently, there are significant differences in the life chances of men and women and in the health status and survival rates of individuals of the same sex. Put simply, men and women with well-paid professional, managerial or technical occupations are more likely to survive to age 65, and to enjoy longer and healthier lives thereafter, than more modestly paid semi-skilled or unskilled workers.

Because pensions would be paid for fewer years, an increase in the state pension age would be equivalent to a cut in benefits. Cutting pension benefits, or shortening the period over which they are paid, would reduce the total amount received by each pensioner. For someone who would have retired at 65 and lived for 20 more years, an increase in the retirement age to 68 would reduce the total value of their pension payments by 12 per cent, assuming benefits are uprated annually by 2.5 per cent. For someone who lives only 15 years after reaching 65, though, the reduction would be more than 17 per cent. Given that a positive correlation exists between income and survival – with the rich living longer on average than the poor – an increase in the retirement age would impact most heavily on those with below-average incomes.

If the state pension age were to rise, private pensions would become even more important than they already are. Incomes from private pensions – whether derived from occupational schemes or individual plans – could be used to offset the reduction in total public pension payments implied by a higher retirement age. In addition, for many people private pensions would constitute the only means by which they could avoid the necessity of remaining in employment beyond the age of 65. As Sections 1.5 and 1.8 point out, though, not everybody has a private pension. Moreover, the best private pension incomes are obtained by workers who enjoy continuous employment in well-paid occupations. Private pensions may, therefore, do little to ameliorate the impact of an increase in the retirement age on those who do least well out of them – low- to middle-income earners in insecure occupations.

While the health of older people has been improving in recent years, improvements have not occurred evenly across the workforce. The greatest advances in the health of those aged 65 and over have been among those at the upper end of the socioeconomic spectrum. Not only do individuals from socio-economic groups IV and V (semi-skilled and unskilled workers) have shorter post 65 life expectancies than those in groups I and II (people with professional and managerial occupations); they also have lower levels of physical fitness. As a result, the obligation to continue in employment beyond the age of 65 would be more physically onerous, as well as more costly, for semi-skilled and unskilled workers than for those with managerial and professional occupations.

Having ruled out a compulsory increase in Britain's state pension age on grounds of fairness, the current government intends instead to adopt a two-pronged approach to longer working lives. First, a key incentive for people to continue in employment on a voluntary basis beyond the official retirement age is to be strengthened. Men aged 65 and women aged 60 currently have the option to postpone collecting their state pension for up to 5 years in return for a 7.5 per cent increase in benefits for each year of postponement. In the next few years, the Government intends to raise the value of this incentive to 10 per cent for each year of pension deferral. Second, unless it can be justified on objective grounds, the practice among some employers of forcing workers to retire when they reach a particular age (e.g. 70) is to be outlawed by 2006.

Employment rates are very low amongst people of retirement age and above. Only 8 per cent of women over state pension age, and 9 per cent of men, are currently in employment (Smeaton and McKay, 2003). The majority are in part-time employment, and most continue working for just a few years after reaching retirement age. Although the outlawing of contractual retirement ages will make it possible for some people who would have been forced to retire to continue working, the numbers involved are small. What is more, given the current vogue for early retirement, it is unlikely that an increase in the benefit enhancement available to those who defer collecting their state pension will do much to boost employment rates amongst people over the age of retirement. Indeed, policies to improve staying-on rates among those in the decade before retirement could have a more positive effect on Britain's public pension finances than those aimed at encouraging continued employment at older ages.

In Britain, as in many other countries, overall labour market participation rates among people in their mid-fifties and early sixties have been in decline for several decades. For an international comparison, see Blundell and Scarpetta (1998). Although participation rates among older women in Britain have remained more or less constant, a dramatic decline has occured in the economic activity of older men. The proportion of males aged 55 to 64 in employment fell from more than 90 per cent in 1968 to less than 70 per cent in 1996. Among men aged 60 to 64, the economic activity rate was more than halved over this period (Blundell and Tanner 1999).

Today's high levels of economic inactivity among older workers (see Table 2.2.1) reflect both unplanned and deliberate withdrawal from employment by those in the 55–64 age group. The post-war expansion of occupational pension scheme membership, described in Section 1.5, has made it possible for large numbers of workers to retire before they reach state pension age. At the same time, unemployment among 55–64-year-olds, who usually bear the brunt of redundancies during times of recession

Table 2.2.1 Economic inactivity rates (%), male and female, by age in May-July
2003

	Age (years)				
	18–24	*25–34*	*35–49*	*50–59 (women)* *50–64 (men)*	*60+ (women)* *65+ (men)*
Women	30.4	25.5	22.2	30.7	90.7
Men	20.6	7.3	7.9	24.9	91.2

Source: Office for National Statistics.

or corporate restructuring, is substantially above the average for all
workers. Raising the level of labour market participation amongst older
workers is now a stated policy objective in the UK (DWP 2002). This has
not always been the case, however.

During the 1970s and much of the 1980s, British governments actively
encouraged the premature exit of older workers from the labour market.
Unemployment was high, especially among young workers, due to economic recession and the large number of baby boomers entering the
labour market. Retiring older workers early was seen as a way to create
job opportunities for the young. From 1977 to 1988, for example, the
government provided subsidies to employers – through the 'Job Release
Scheme' – who replaced employees who were nearing state pension age
with younger, unemployed workers. Policies like this stood in marked contrast to the approach taken in the aftermath of World War II. In the 1950s
and 1960s, labour was in short supply and the economy was booming.
Against this background, employers were encouraged to retain their older
workers for as long as possible.

In the late 1980s, growing concern about the economic consequences of
population ageing caused the government to reappraise its employment
policies. Raising the economic activity rates of older workers became a
priority once more. In 1988 the Job Release Scheme was scrapped. It was
replaced with the 'Fifty-Plus Jobstart' initiative, which aimed to get older
unemployed workers into part-time employment. Since then, various advi-
sory groups have been formed, and codes of practice published, aimed at
tackling age discrimination in the workplace. In 1999, the 'New Deal' for
older workers was launched, which provides a financial incentive for
unemployed workers over the age of 50 to get back into employment.

Proposals for further measures to raise employment levels among
workers in their fifties and early sixties were set out in the Green Paper
(DWP 2002). In line with the approach taken since 1988, future policies
would focus on getting unemployed workers aged 50 and over back into
employment and on promoting increased retention of older workers by
employers. The Green Paper announced the setting up of pilot schemes to
assist recipients of incapacity benefits (see Table 2.2.2) to get back to

Table 2.2.2 Percentage of all economically inactive people of working age registered as long-term sick or disabled in spring 2003

	Age (years)			
	16–24	*25–34*	*35–49*	*50–59/64*
Males	4	40	60	42
Females	3	8	25	35

Source: Barham (2003).

work. For some time the government had suspected that large numbers of
individuals who were nearing state pension age were, in effect, retiring
early by moving out of work and onto incapacity benefits. The Green
Paper also set out the government's intention to raise by five years the
normal retirement age for new entrants to public sector schemes and to
consult with private sector employers on proposals for employees to be
able to draw occupational pensions whilst continuing to work for the sponsoring firm.

An increase in the economic activity rates of older workers would have
an immediate and positive impact on Britain's public pension finances.
With more people in their fifties and early sixties in employment, the flow
of funds into the state pension scheme would rise, because NI contributions must be paid by all employees below retirement age whose earned
incomes are above the lower earnings limit. Smeaton and McKay (2003)
have shown that individuals who held jobs just before reaching retirement
age were those most likely to be in employment thereafter. This suggests
that the government's desire to see more people working beyond retirement age might also be fulfilled if higher levels of economic activity at
older ages can be brought about through a reduction in the numbers
leaving the labour market early.

Important differences have been observed in the retirement behaviour
of workers who have occupational pensions and those who do not (Blundell and Tanner 1999). Employees with defined benefit occupational pensions are less likely to leave employment before their scheme's retirement
age – typically 60 – but they are more likely to do so thereafter. It does not
follow, however, that the numbers of people retiring early could be
reduced via a statutory increase in the minimum age at which occupational
pensions may be drawn. Such a move would provoke outrage in the workforce. Moreover, without a compensating reduction in accrual rates, it
would make DB schemes more expensive to provide, especially if residual
life expectancy continues to rise rapidly. Scheme closures would undoubtedly follow, with employers offering cheaper money purchase plans in
their place.

Although a reduction in accrual rates could preserve the affordability of

DB schemes, it would make membership less attractive. As a result, large numbers of workers might be expected to opt for individual money purchase plans instead, which permit pensions to be taken from the age of 50. Increasing the minimum age at which pensions may be drawn from individual DC schemes would almost certainly be costly in terms of the government's wider pensions objectives. The amounts contributed to these plans, and the numbers of workers contributing, would likely fall, rather than rise as the government would like to see. Thus, as long as participation in private schemes remains voluntary, an increase in their minimum pension ages is not really an option. On the other hand, removing the incentive to retire early currently provided by the tax-privileged status of private pension incomes is.

In Britain, the tax treatment of pensions in payment is much more generous than that applied to earned incomes. Pension payments, like earned incomes, are subject to income tax at an individual's marginal rate. Unlike earnings from employment, however, pensions in payment are exempt from National Insurance contributions, which, because they are compulsory, can be thought of as another income tax. At the time of writing (September 2003), NICs are levied at a rate of 11 per cent of eligible earnings below the UEL and 1 per cent thereafter. By exempting pensions in payment from NICs, the tax system effectively subsidises retirement, including early retirement. It is currently possible for an individual to retire at 60 with an occupational pension equal to two-thirds of their pre-tax earnings, but with a post-tax income which is not much below what they were able to obtain from employment.

A good case can be made for exempting the pensions of those over state retirement age from National Insurance contributions. After all, as well as earning public pension entitlements, NICs buy cover against a range of contingencies that retirees do not face – e.g. unemployment and industrial injury. An exemption which distorts labour market behaviour by providing a financial incentive for early retirement is, on the other hand, much harder to justify. Removing the NIC exemption on the private pensions of individuals below state pension age would improve the public pension finances through increased National Insurance receipts. By eliminating an incentive for early retirement, it would also help to improve the economic activity rates of older workers.

2.3 OF PONZI SCHEMES AND PENSION FUNDS

PAYG pension schemes are often characterised as Ponzi schemes, so called after the Boston swindler Charles Ponzi. Like the pyramid investment schemes invented by Ponzi – an Italian immigrant to early twentieth century America – which rely on the income from new investors to pay those who joined earlier, PAYG schemes finance the pensions of former workers from the contributions of those currently in employment. As long as each new group of investors is larger than the previous one, Ponzi schemes permit members to get back much more than they put in. Problems arise, though, when increasing numbers of new investors cannot be found. Promised pay-outs will be reneged upon and, ultimately, these schemes collapse.

The story of Ida May Fuller, the first person to receive a social security pension in America, is sometimes cited as evidence of the Ponzi nature of PAYG public pension schemes (Carter and Shipman 1996, Wallace 1999). Fuller, a legal secretary from Ludlow, Vermont, died on 27 January 1975 aged 100. Known affectionately as 'Aunt Ida', she famously received pension benefits worth some $23,000, having paid just $22 in social security contributions. Her first monthly pension cheque, received on 31 January 1940, was for $22.54. Periodic cost of living increases over the 35 years of her retirement – the first being for $18.75 in 1951 – steadily raised the value of Aunt Ida's pension payments. The last cheque she received was for $109.20.

In 1940 there were more than 40 American workers financing the pensions of each retired person. By 1951, the support ratio – the ratio of workers to pensioners – had fallen to 16. When Aunt Ida died, in 1975, the support ratio stood at just 3.2. As the number of contributors supporting each retired person declined, contributions had to rise in order to maintain benefit levels. In 1940 the combined employee and employer contribution rate was set at 2 per cent of earnings. It rose to 3 per cent in 1950, 6 per cent in 1960, 10 per cent in 1980 and has stood at 12 per cent since 1988 (Feldstein 1996). This increase in contribution rates illustrates an important difference between Ponzi schemes and PAYG pensions. Unlike Ponzi, who had to rely on ever larger numbers of individuals joining his scheme voluntarily, governments can and do make participation in PAYG pension schemes compulsory, and can force new entrants to contribute more than those who joined earlier.

An initial decline in the support ratio is, in fact, a feature of all PAYG pension schemes. As the number of individuals retiring each year is added to the total of surviving retirees, the ratio of workers to pensioners will fall, even where the workforce is growing. In the absence of population shocks, the support ratio will eventually stabilise at a level determined by prevailing fertility and survival rates. Because of earnings growth, however, pension benefits can rise even where the support ratio is constant over time. Thus, PAYG schemes can deliver a positive rate of return to contributors, where each generation of retirees is able to receive higher pension payments than it provided for the preceding generation. Together, Samuelson (1958) and Aaron (1966) have shown that, with contributions equal to a fixed fraction of earned incomes, the rate of return to PAYG schemes is given by the sum of the rates of growth of the workforce and average earnings. In other words, the rate of return to PAYG schemes equals the rate of growth of total earnings.

As Section 1.4 notes, zero or negative rates of growth are projected for the workforces of developed countries over the coming decades. Consequently, unless contribution rates rise, the rate of return provided by PAYG pension schemes will be at or below the rate of growth of earnings. Since the mid-1970s earnings growth in developed countries has averaged 2 to 3 per cent a year, and is not expected to rise significantly in the future. Stock markets, on the other hand, have the potential to deliver annual rates of return significantly greater than 2 or 3 per cent, despite their disastrous performance since September 2000. In the 1980s and 1990s, for example, share values in Europe rose, on average, by 10 per cent a year in real terms. Even if the recent sharp decline in share values marks the start of a period of more modest increases, equity returns might reasonably be expected to out-perform earnings growth over the medium to long term by a margin of 5 or 6 per cent a year.

The likelihood that stock market returns will exceed the returns to PAYG pensions by a considerable margin in the future suggests that contributors to public pension schemes would be better off if their contributions were allowed to accumulate in a fund which was invested mainly in equities rather than being used to pay current pensioners. Indeed, the potential for portfolio investments to deliver higher returns than PAYG schemes is one reason why Feldstein (1996), Carter and Shipman (1996) and others have argued for the privatisation of public pensions. The arguments of the privatisers, however, really boil down to a debate about the superiority of funding over PAYG financing rather than a case for privatisation *per se*. There is no theoretical reason why private pension providers should be better than governments at managing funded pensions. Publicly administered funds may actually be preferable if the costs of private provision are higher due to a lack of scale economies and the need to engage in expensive marketing activities.

The case for substituting funding (where workers save for their own pensions) for PAYG pensions (where they pay for somebody else's pension) can be summarised as follows. PAYG schemes are Ponzi schemes which, given adverse demographics, offer contributors very poor value for money. Funded pensions have the potential to provide higher retirement incomes due to the superior rate of return on portfolio investments. PAYG schemes should, therefore, be wound up, with funded schemes set up to replace them. Funding could lead to increased investment and faster economic growth by raising national savings rates. Moreover, substituting funding for PAYG financing would eliminate the need for current and future generations of workers to stump up more in taxes as national populations age.

Some of the presumed benefits of funding over PAYG financing are at best questionable. For example, as Davis (1995) observes, some countries (e.g. Britain and America) with very high levels of pension funding have very low savings ratios, while other countries (e.g Italy) have high rates of saving but low levels of pension funding. Likewise, a move to fully funded pensions would only obviate the need for current and future workers to pay more in taxes as populations age if the provision of PAYG-financed retirement benefits was the only form of state support for the elderly. On the other hand, it is almost certainly the case that the rate of return to PAYG schemes will remain well below that of portfolio investments during the coming decades. Nevertheless, the existence of transition costs means that a move from PAYG to funded pensions may not be advantageous, even if the rate of return to funding is higher.

Transition costs arise because to move from PAYG financing to fully funded pensions creates a double generational burden. PAYG pension payments will need to continue for those who are already retired or who, at the time the switch is made, do not have sufficient working years left to save for their own pensions. For several decades, then, some workers will have to save for their own retirement while continuing to provide other people with PAYG pensions. These workers might, therefore, be expected to make their resentment felt at the ballot box. To make the transition to funding more politically acceptable, governments could finance part or all of their PAYG pension commitments by issuing bonds. Since this debt would ultimately have to be repaid, though, a bond-financed transition simply spreads the pain over a longer period. The fact is, once a PAYG scheme has been established it is not possible to replace it with funding without making some individuals worse off.

It is plausible that a switch from PAYG financing to funding could make future generations better off than they would otherwise be. The gains to future generations would, however, come at considerable cost to the transition generation. The more generous the PAYG scheme that is being replaced, and the more rapid the rate of population ageing, the higher will be the transition costs. Moreover, limits on borrowing may reduce governments' ability to spread the pain over successive generations. For example, the Growth and Stability Pact, adopted by European countries which have introduced the Euro as their common currency, restricts annual government borrowing to just 3 per cent of national income. As Miles (1998) points out, if the switch from PAYG financing to funding creates losers as well as winners, the losses may be large enough and sufficiently widespread to make the change either undesirable or impracticable.

The privatisation of pensions in Latin America is often held up as evidence of the practicability of moving from PAYG financing to funding. As Section 1.5 notes, in 1981 Chile closed its PAYG public pension scheme and replaced it with a system of privately administered, compulsory, individual funded pensions. Instead of paying their predecessors' pensions, Chilean workers now contribute 10 per cent of their earnings to their own pension fund and use the accumulated balance to purchase an indexed annuity at retirement. Like other Latin American countries which have subsequently moved, or are in the process of moving, away from PAYG financing in favour of funding, Chile chose to spread the transition costs over current and future generations by financing its outstanding PAYG obligations through borrowing. Since the interest payments on the debt, as well as the repayment of principal, comes out of general taxation, the transition costs, in the form of higher taxes, are borne by pensioners and workers alike.

The apparent ease with which Chile, Mexico, Bolivia and several other Latin American countries were able to replace their PAYG schemes with funded pensions may not be replicated elsewhere. In the 1980s, Latin American countries faced a different set of circumstances from those prevailing in many developed countries today. PAYG pensions were at relatively low levels and there were lots of young and few old people (Boldrin *et al.* 1999). In the United States and Europe, where outstanding PAYG commitments are larger and dependency ratios are higher, the burden associated with a transition to funding would be much greater. What is more, even if the costs of switching to funded pensions were low, such a switch would only be worth making in the absence of a superior alternative.

PAYG and funded pensions have different characteristics which mean that they are not perfect substitutes. PAYG pensions are labour-market based, whereas funded pensions are financial-market based. The rate of return to PAYG pensions depends upon the rate of growth of total earnings. The rate of return to pension funds is determined by the returns available on a range of financial assets, but mainly equities. Although equity returns have been, and are likely to remain, above the rate of growth of earnings, they are much more volatile. The returns to PAYG pensions may be lower, but they are more stable. In the debate over funding versus PAYG, then, the argument is about the relative merits of moving from a low-return, low-risk approach to pension provision to one where the returns are potentially higher but the risks are greater. The either/or nature of the debate thus takes no account of the possibility that a mixed approach to pension provision might be preferable to exclusive reliance on PAYG or funding.

The case for providing retirement incomes through a combination of PAYG financed and funded pensions derives from the fact that PAYG and funding have different risk/return characteristics. Essentially, the argument is that workers would do best not to put all their retirement eggs in the same basket. By contributing to PAYG schemes as well as funded pensions, workers can take advantage of the benefits available from both. The lower but more certain returns from PAYG schemes can be set against the greater risk associated with the higher returns to funding. Moreover, variations in the rates of return to PAYG and funding tend to be negatively correlated. Thus, a mix of PAYG and funded pensions could be expected to deliver superior retirement incomes to those available from

PAYG or funding alone. If PAYG and funding are viewed as complementary assets in the same retirement income portfolio, the issue is not whether one approach is preferable to the other, but in what propor tions they should be combined.

It is sometimes argued that funded schemes are preferable to PAYG pensions because they are less susceptible to political risk, especially where they are privately administered. The suggestion is that levels of contributions to or benefits from funded schemes are somehow less vulnerable to changes arising from the politically motivated actions – or inaction – of governments. There is, however, a considerable degree of political risk associated with both PAYG and funding. PAYG schemes may appear more susceptible to political risk, though, because their parameters – the contribution rate, benefit formula, method of indexation and retirement age – are set directly by governments. Faced with rising pension costs, governments may jeopardise the solvency of a PAYG scheme by failing to take the necessary remedial action. They may be unwilling to cut benefits or raise contributions for fear of alienating a large section of the electorate.

In fact, politicians can just as easily undermine the performance, and even the solvency, of funded schemes. For example, in the wake of a scandal like the Maxwell affair, discussed in Section 2.6, a government might introduce hasty and ill-advised changes to the rules governing funded schemes so as to be seen to be doing something by the electorate. Alternatively, politicians may fail to take effective action to safeguard members' funds where, because of pension scheme abuses, it is desirable that they should. Governments might be tempted to raid pension fund assets by imposing special taxes on them, or removing their tax privileges, in order to be able to reduce general taxation. They may also seek to create a guaranteed market for their own sovereign debt by requiring pension funds to allocate a large proportion of their assets to government bonds.

2.4 TAXING FUNDED PRIVATE PENSIONS

Taxation is a major determinant of the performance of private funded pensions. Other important determinants – discussed in Sections 1.7 and 2.8 of this book – are funding, accounting and investment rules. The level of taxation and the way in which taxes are applied will influence the rate at which pension savings accumulate and, hence, the amount of retirement income that private pensions can deliver. The absence of a favourable tax regime may be one reason for the low level of development of private pensions in a number of countries. A generous tax treatment can make private pensions more attractive to providers as well as contributors and enhance their political acceptability as substitutes for public pensions. On the other hand, providing private pensions with tax privileges has revenue implications for governments and may have undesirable redistributive effects.

The taxation of moneys flowing through private pension schemes may be undertaken on either a comprehensive income tax or an expenditure tax basis. A comprehensive income tax regime taxes all income equally – earnings as well as returns to investment – as it is received. Under an expenditure tax regime, tax is levied at the point where income is consumed. A key distinction between the two approaches is in their impact on the returns to saving. With an expenditure tax the pre-tax and post-tax returns to saving are the same, whereas post-tax returns are lower than pre-tax returns under a comprehensive income tax. Economists are generally agreed that an expenditure tax is the appropriate tax regime for private pensions (Dilnot and Johnson 1993, Davis 1995, Booth and Cooper 2002). This is the approach adopted in the UK.

In practice, whether private pensions are taxed on an expenditure tax or a comprehensive income tax basis depends upon the point or points at which taxation occurs. With funded pensions there are three points at which taxation may be applied: when contributions are made, when investment returns are earned and when retirement benefits are received. There are, therefore, eight possible ways to tax pensions, ranging from no taxation at any point to taxing at all three points. To simplify the analysis a convenient notation has emerged within the pensions taxation literature, where the letters E and T are used to denote points which are exempt from tax or where taxes are applied. Thus, TTE is a shorthand way of saying that taxes are levied on pension contributions and investment returns, but income in the form of pension benefits is exempt from taxation. In other words, TTE is a comprehensive income tax.

There are two possible expenditure tax regimes for private pensions: EET and TEE. In both cases investment returns are exempt from taxation and income is taxed once, when it is drawn under EET and when it is contributed with TEE. Consequently, under either regime the pre-tax and post-tax returns to pension saving will be equal. This contrasts with the two possible comprehensive income tax regimes, TTE and ETT, where the taxation of investment returns means that post-tax returns are always lower than pre-tax returns. TTE and ETT provide a disincentive to save, since, under these regimes, immediate consumption is worth more than consumption in the future. EET and TEE, however, are both neutral with respect to immediate or future consumption. With a tax rate of 22 per cent, £100 of taxable income could be used immediately to purchase consumption of £78. Alternatively, £100 could be saved for a year, earning a return of say 6 per cent. This would permit £82.68 of consumption at the end of the year ($£100 \times 1.06 \times 78$). The extra £4.68 of consumption available after one year is the possible return sacrificed in order to have £78 of immediate consumption ($£78 \times 1.06 = £82.68$).

Although EET and TEE are both expenditure taxes, and hence appropriate regimes for the taxation of private pensions, EET has some practical advantages over TEE. Under TEE, tax relief is granted in the future rather than being immediate. As Davis (1995) observes, the possibility exists, therefore, that future governments may renege. Thus, saving for retirement may be less attractive under TEE than it is under EET. In addition, while the value of retirement saving net of taxation is the same under both regimes, because taxation is deferred to the future larger balances will accumulate under EET. For example, with a tax rate of 22 per cent, contributions of £100 invested for 10 years with a 6 per cent compound rate of return would yield a fund value of £179.08 under EET, but only £139.69 under TEE.

The taxation of private pensions under the EET regime – as in the UK – creates a tax expenditure for the government. Because the tax liability is on pension benefits that will be paid in the future rather than on contributions made now, governments forego an amount of current tax revenue. In Britain, the intertemporal shift in tax liability is only partial, though, since money contributed by employees (but not employers) to a private pension is still subject to National Insurance contributions and, as Section 1.7 notes, not all investment returns are tax free. In 2001–2002, the tax expenditure on UK private pensions was around £12 billion. Since this money will be recouped by a future government, it represents a substantial transfer of income from current to future taxpayers. EET results in current tax rates being higher and future tax rates being lower than they would otherwise need to be for a given level of government spending and borrowing. Moreover, because EET leads to larger accumulated funds, due to tax deferral, there is also a transfer of income to individuals who have an occupational pension (usually more affluent workers) from those who do not (typically, low-income earners).

To limit the scale of the tax expenditure associated with the EET regime, British governments have placed limits on the annual amounts that may be contributed to private pensions. In the fiscal year 2002–2003, for example, contributions by individuals and/or their employers to DC plans were restricted to £3,600 or an age-related proportion of earnings – from 17.5 to 40 per cent – whichever is the greater. Employee contributions to a DB scheme were limited to 15 per cent of earnings. While there were no explicit limits on contributions from employers, Booth and Cooper (2002) note that limits on scheme benefits and funding levels effectively cap total contributions.

Because part of the funds accrued in UK private pension schemes may be taken as a tax-free lump sum, there is scope for tax avoidance under the EET regime. As Blake (1992) points out, were it not for the tax-free status of lump sum withdrawals, the EET regime would simply be a mechanism for tax deferral. As well as limiting the size of tax expenditures on private pensions, contribution ceilings also limit the extent to which tax avoidance is possible. In addition, they reduce the scope for tax arbitrage. When pension contributions are taxed at the contributor's marginal rate, as they are in the UK, EET makes it possible for individuals to transfer part of their tax liability during their working years (when they face a high marginal rate of taxation) to their retirement years (when their marginal tax rate will be lower) by contributing to a private pension.

There are two groups of workers for whom annual limits on the amount of tax-free contributions to private pensions are especially problematic: individuals with fluctuating incomes and late starters. Workers whose incomes vary over time may need to reduce their pension contributions in years when their earnings are relatively low, and increase them in higher earning years. They may be unable to do this efficiently, though, if the amount of contributions needed in higher-earning years is above the permitted maximum. Those who start a private pension comparatively late in life, and thus have a relatively short time in which to build up a retirement fund, may also be frustrated by the annual contribution limit. Proposed changes contained in the 2002 pensions Green Paper (DWP 2002) should alleviate these problems. The Green Paper proposes that the annual contribution limit should be raised to £200,000, with a lifetime cap of £1.4 million. These changes would come into effect in 2004.

The tax treatment of private pensions in Britain and other countries where they operate is much more generous than that applied to other savings vehicles. For example, a comprehensive income tax of the TTE form is applied to UK bank and building society accounts. Deposits and interest earned are taxed, while withdrawals are tax free. Although an expenditure tax is applied to TESSAs (tax exempt special savings accounts) and ISAs (individual savings accounts), it is of the less advantageous TEE form. In general, the differential tax treatment of savings vehicles should lead individuals to prefer the most tax-favoured vehicle. Differences in the characteristics of alternative forms of saving, however, will limit the extent to which tax differences distort savings behaviour. The relative tax disadvantages of non-pension savings are offset by the greater choice these vehicles offer savers over the size and timing of withdrawals.

In countries like Britain, where the level of income replacement provided by public pensions is low, the exceptionally generous tax treatment of private pension saving is often justified on paternalistic grounds. To ensure that they have adequate resources in retirement, people require an incentive to make their own private pension provision. In addition, because part of the state's support for the elderly in Britain is income-related, a favourable tax environment for private pensions is also justified as a way of reducing the future cost to taxpayers of means-tested retirement benefits. Dilnot *et al.* (1994) argue, however, that granting private pensions tax privileges is not necessarily the most effective way to ensure adequacy of retirement incomes or to reduce the future tax cost of means-tested retirement benefits. Tax incentives may be of little value to individuals with modest incomes. Improved state provision may be a more effective way of ensuring that they have adequate resources in retirement. Moreover, even if tax privileges promote increased pension saving among the better-off, the future saving to the exchequer may turn out to be less than the immediate tax expenditure.

Another argument for treating private pensions more favourably than other forms of saving is that because pension schemes are long term savings vehicles their special tax status will raise the general level of saving in the economy. High returns arising from the tax subsidy will induce individuals to substitute immediate consumption with consumption in the future. This in turn will have a positive effect on the rates of investment and economic growth. A higher level of overall saving will not occur, though, if the substitution effect of the tax privileges is matched by the income effect. The income effect arises because, due to higher returns, individuals do not need to save as much to reach a given level of savings. Indeed, aggregate private saving may actually fall if, due to the tax privilege, individuals can achieve their target level of retirement income by saving less than they would otherwise need to save. If the substitution effect outweighs the income effect, and private saving increases, this could be offset by a reduction in government saving due to lower tax revenues. Furthermore, tax privileges may simply alter the composition of saving. Money that would in any case have gone to other savings vehicles may go to pensions instead. In this case, there will be no effect on total saving. A study by Engen *et al.* (1996) found that tax incentives had a strong effect on the allocation of saving, but little or no effect on its level. Davis (1995) cites research which also suggests that if tax advantages do have a positive impact on aggregate saving, the effect is rather small.

An important aspect of the special tax treatment of private pensions concerns the taxation of earned incomes and income received as pension benefits. Income from private pensions is tax-favoured because, unlike earnings from employment, it is not subject to National Insurance contributions. Consequently, the post-tax reduction in income for someone retiring before state retirement age – when earnings are also exempted from NICs – is substantially less than it would be if both forms of income attracted the same level of total taxation. Thus, the preferential tax treatment afforded to private pension incomes provides a heightened incentive for early retirement. This lack of fiscal neutrality between normal and early retirement is at odds with the present government's aim, stated in the 2002 pensions Green Paper, of encouraging people to work for longer. Yet, the Green Paper contains no proposals to equalise the tax treatment of earnings and pension incomes. The revenue implications of early retirement for public pensions are discussed in Section 2.2.

2.5 ANNUITIES AND ANNUITISATION

An annuity can be thought of as a life insurance policy in reverse. With life insurance, policy-holders make a stream of payments to an insurance company until they die. Upon their death, the insurer makes a lump sum payment to the beneficiaries of the policy. An annuity is a contract which entitles a person to receive regular cash payments for as long as they live, in return for an initial lump sum payment to an insurance company. Because annuity payments are guaranteed for life, purchasers of annuities are buying insurance against the risk of out-living their retirement savings. Although annuities may be purchased voluntarily, in many countries, including the UK, Denmark, Sweden and the Netherlands, annuitisation of part or all of the funds accrued in DC plans is compulsory.

Annuities have a long history. Contracts similar to modern temporary annuities were available in Roman times. Known as *annua*, these contracts entitled individuals to receive a stream of payments for a limited period in return for a single up-front payment. Poterba (2001) notes that single-premium life annuities were available in the Middle Ages, and that in seventeenth century France annuity pools known as *tontines* were in operation. In the eighteenth century, some governments, including the British government, sold annuities in order to raise funds. It was also in the eighteenth century that the modern annuity market emerged, with annuities being sold by private insurance companies (Poterba 2001).

Unlike the early government annuities – which, in Britain, originally offered the same annual income to all purchasers irrespective of their age or sex – today's private annuity contracts are sophisticated financial products. The incomes they provide vary between annuitants according to their personal circumstances at the time of purchase and the type of contract they buy. In general, annuity rates – the value of annual income payments expressed as a proportion of the initial lump sum – are higher for men than women. They are also higher for older annuitants of both sexes than they are for those who annuitise at a younger age. While some annuities are very straightforward products, offering a fixed nominal income until death, others offer incomes which rise in real terms over time or continue paying after the annuitant's death. Some annuity contracts even make it possible for purchasers to take on a degree of investment risk in order to benefit from rising asset values.

The main types of annuity contract available in the UK fall into three broad categories: level annuities, increasing annuities and variable or investment-linked annuities (Stark and Curry 2001). Level annuities are fixed-rate products which pay the same nominal income every year. They are simple to understand, and offer the best initial annuity rates. This is probably why the vast majority of annuity purchases are for level annuities even though they fail to protect annuitants from the effects of inflation. Because the income they pay is fixed in nominal terms, over time inflation

Table 2.5.1 Declining real value of level annuity payments over a 30-year period with 2.5, 3 and 5 per cent inflation

Inflation (%)	Time (years)					
	5	10	15	20	25	30
2.5	88.11	77.63	68.40	60.27	53.10	46.79
3	85.87	73.74	63.33	54.38	46.70	40.10
5	77.38	59.87	46.33	35.85	27.74	21.46

Source: Author's calculations.

erodes the real value of level annuity payments. As Table 2.5.1 shows, the effects of even a fairly low rate of inflation can reduce substantially the real value of annuity pay-outs for longer-lived individuals. With inflation averaging just 2.5 per cent a year, after 20 years the real value of level annuity payments will be cut by almost 40 per cent.

Increasing annuities offer full or partial inflation proofing, albeit at a cost to the annuitant. They are either indexed or escalating. Pay-outs from indexed annuities rise or fall in line with changes in some index of inflation (e.g. the UK's retail price index), thereby maintaining the real value of annuity payments. The protected rights portion of contracted-out money purchase plans in the UK must be used to purchase an annuity offering limited price indexation – up to 5 per cent per annum. A distinction between fully indexed annuities and those offering limited price indexation is that the nominal income from the latter cannot be reduced if retail prices fall. Because indexed annuities are backed with index-linked bonds, which are more expensive than the fixed-interest bonds used to back level annuities, their initial payments are lower.

Whereas changes in the nominal value of income from an indexed annuity are variable, escalating annuities offer a guaranteed annual rate of increase, normally 3 or 5 per cent. Thus, escalating annuities provide full inflation-proofing up to the escalation rate, and partial protection for higher rates. Moreover, in years when the rate of inflation is below the value of the escalator, owners of escalating annuities will see the real value of their incomes rise. Nominal annuity rates are, however, initially much lower for escalating annuities than for level annuities, and catching up can take many years. For example, with a discount of 30 per cent, it would take 7 years and 12 years respectively for the nominal income from a 5 or 3 per cent escalating annuity to rise to that provided by a level annuity.

Compared with level and increasing annuity contracts, investment-linked annuities are relatively new. They provide variable income which depends upon the performance of an underlying with-profits or unit-linked fund. Like escalating annuities, they provide a degree of inflation hedging. In addition, because they are linked to equities rather than bonds, they have the potential to deliver superior rates of real income growth. Since equity values can go down as well as up, though, the income from these products can also fall. Thus they are more risky than most other types of annuity, although investment-linked annuities often have a guaranteed minimum income level. The income from unit-linked annuities is particularly volatile because, unlike with-profits annuities, there is no smoothing of investment returns. Investment-linked annuities are also more expensive to administer and hence usually offer lower starting incomes.

The annuity rates offered by insurers vary in line with changes in long-term interest rates. This is because in order to provide an income which is guaranteed for life, insurers invest annuitants' funds in risk-free government bonds. In the UK these bonds are known as gilt-edged securities, or gilts for short. Like any insurance product, annuities work by pooling risk. The funds invested by annuitants who die early are used to subsidise the incomes of those who live a long time. Because of this mortality cross-subsidy, annuitants are able to receive a better rate of return than they could get from investing in gilts directly.

A distinction exists, however, between the annuity rates payable to individuals and those available on annuities in general. Individual rates differ between annuitants, reflecting differences in their actuarial circumstances (Table 2.5.2). The higher rates paid to men reflect their lower life expectancies. Although women typically receive lower annuity rates than male annuitants of the same age, they can expect to be paid for longer. These gender differences in rates mean that the value of an annuity contract – the amount of income received for a given lump sum payment – will, on average, be the same for both sexes. Younger annuitants of both sexes receive lower rates than older ones for the same reason. Impaired-life annuities paying above-average rates can be purchased by the terminally ill, smokers, and other individuals with diminished life expectancies.

For most people, private annuities have historically played a minor role in retirement income provision. Even though their significance has grown in recent years, annuities currently account for only 10 per cent of average pensioner income in the UK. The growing trend for employers to offer

Table 2.5.2 Typical annuity rates, November 2003

	M55	F50	M60	F55	M65	F60	M70	F65
Level	5.84	5.22	6.57	5.64	7.50	6.23	9.05	7.03
Escalating 3%	3.91	3.23	4.66	3.67	5.71	4.26	7.14	5.07
RPI	4.05	3.36	4.77	3.79	5.79	4.36	7.23	5.14

Source: Annuities Online.

Notes
M = male.
F = female.

defined contribution rather than defined benefit pension schemes and the growth of personal saving for retirement means, however, that private annuities are set to become much more important from now on. Yet, these products are widely perceived to lack flexibility and to offer poor value for money. Consequently, there is considerable hostility in the UK to the legal requirement for contributors to tax-favoured DC plans to annuitise most of their pension savings.

Compulsory annuitisation of funds in DC plans can be justified on several grounds. The first is paternalism. Without compulsion, individuals may not act in their own best interests. Thus compulsion is justified in order to prevent individuals from spending their retirement savings too quickly or, perhaps, from blowing the lot on luxury holidays. It is often argued that governments have a right to act paternalistically, since the funds accruing in DC schemes derive, in part, from public money given in the form of tax relief on pension contributions. Compulsory annuitisation is also seen as a way to protect taxpayers from exploitation. This is because the potential for double-dipping exists where there is no mandatory requirement for annuitisation. If retirees know that taxpayers are willing to support the elderly poor, they will have an incentive to play the system by running down their retirement savings – on which they have received tax relief – to a level where they become eligible to receive means-tested benefits.

In Britain, hostility to compulsory annuitisation has, in recent years, been fuelled by falling annuity rates. These were halved between 1995 and 2000. Underlying this reduction in annuity rates was a substantial fall in gilt yields. The yield on long-dated gilts fell from 8.35 per cent in 1995 to 4.98 per cent in 2000, as governments sought to borrow less and repay some of their outstanding debt. With annuity rates at a historic low, critics of compulsory annuitisation argued that annuitants were being forced to invest in financial products which offered poor value for money. This argument is weak, however, because it fails to take account of other factors relating to the value for money of financial contracts. These include the term of the contract, the risks borne by the purchaser and the cost of supplying it.

Bond yields are not the sole determinant of annuity rates. Life expectancy is also relevant. If annuitants live longer, they will have to be paid for longer. Thus, to compensate for rising life expectancy, insurers will reduce the annuity rates they offer. Against a background of increasing longevity, therefore, declining annuity rates do not automatically imply that the value for money of annuities is falling. Likewise, if the rate of return on annuities is lower than that available from other forms of investment, it does not necessarily mean that these products give poor value for money. The absence of risk is an important aspect of the value of an annuity. Other forms of investment may offer higher returns, but they also carry the risk of capital loss. The lower return on annuities reflects the fact that the income they provide is guaranteed for life.

Low annuity rates would suggest poor value for money if they resulted from insurers having to cover high costs of supplying annuities. The costs of supplying annuities arise from insurers' need to cover administrative expenses such as marketing and investment costs, commissions to agents, salaries and overheads, and from adverse selection. Insurers face adverse selection because annuitants typically have longer life expectancies than the average for the population as a whole. For example, Poterba (2001) reports that in 1998 the probability of a 65-year-old man randomly selected from the general population dying within a year of his 65th birthday was 2.21. This compared with probabilities of just 1.53 and 0.89 respectively for equivalent purchasers of compulsory and voluntary annuities. Voluntary annuity purchases are mainly confined to wealthy individuals, and, as Section 2.2 shows, the rich tend to have longer than average life expectancies. Although compulsory annuitisation reduces adverse selection it cannot eliminate it altogether as long as individuals are free to choose not to contribute to a DC plan.

Adverse selection is costly for insurers because it reduces their ability to pool mortality risk. It therefore induces them to charge more for annuities than would be charged if adverse selection was not present. A study by Murthi *et al.* (1999) found that adverse selection accounted for the majority of annuity costs for the typical individual, possibly as much as two-thirds. Overall, the study found that total annuity costs for the typical individual were around 10 per cent of the annuitised sum. In other words, annuity payments were about 10 per cent below what would be available on a costless annuity, given anticipated mortality rates and the prevailing yield structure of risk-free government bonds.

A widely used measure of the value for money of annuities is the money's worth ratio (Friedman and Warshawsky 1990, Murthi *et al.* 1999, Poterba 2001). The money's worth ratio (MWR) of an annuity is the sum of the present value of discounted payments for the typical annuitant divided by its initial cost. An MWR of 1 would be the actuarially fair value, where the present value of discounted payments equals the sum invested. In practice, values of less than 1 will be observed, because annuity providers must cover their costs and earn a profit. Poterba (2001) calculates that the MWR for compulsory purchase annuities for men and women aged 65 in May 2000 were respectively 0.971 and 0.975. He also cites estimates showing that the MWR on the average compulsory annuity in the UK fell from 0.996 in 1990 to 0.905 in 1999.

The relatively small number of compulsory annuitants who exercise their open market option (OMO) suggests that some individuals may not be getting the best-value annuities available to them. The OMO is the right of annuitants to purchase an annuity from a different insurer from the one providing their DC plan. Differences in the rates offered by annuity providers mean that it often pays to shop around. Yet, Stark and Curry (2001) cite estimates of between 20 and 45 per cent for the proportion of all compulsory annuitants who exercise their OMO. While annuitants with small fund values may be prevented from shopping around because insurers often set a minimum premium for external annuities – i.e. annuity purchases where the terminal fund was accumulated with a different insurer – other annuitants are almost certainly ignorant of the option to shop around. In addition to improvements in the information given to pension plan holders, proposals for promoting greater use of the OMO include a legal requirement for plan providers to make annuitants aware of the three best options available to them in the open market.

Whilst it is possible to draw comparisons between the rates of return and charges on annuities and other financial products, what constitutes value for money is ultimately a subjective judgement which depends upon annuitants' individual time preferences and levels of risk aversion. The other major criticism of the current compulsory annuitisation regime – that it is too rigid – can be analysed more objectively. The issue at stake is whether, in order to achieve its goals, the current regime places unnecessary or costly constraints on annuitants' freedom of action. The goals of compulsory annuitisation are threefold: to insure that public moneys accumulating in DC schemes are used to secure a private pension, to prevent poverty in old age, and to limit the overall level of demand for tax-financed, means-tested, retirement benefits.

In fact, there is considerable flexibility within the compulsory annuitization regime. As Stark and Curry (2001, 2002) show, many of the alleged failings of the current arrangements are really problems of perception born out of a lack of understanding. For example, it is widely believed that, by forcing people to part with their pension savings, compulsory annuitisation prevents annuitants from bequeathing their un-consumed pension wealth to their heirs. Leaving aside the moot question of whether it should be a function of pension schemes to facilitate wealth transfers from one generation to the next, there is, in reality, a strong element of inheritability in the current annuitisation rules.

It was noted in Section 1.5 that 25 per cent of the funds accumulated in UK defined contribution plans may be taken as a tax-free lump sum. Thus, a quarter of DC pension savings are immediately available for bequests. In addition, beyond the obligation to purchase an annuity providing limited price indexation to cover the protected rights portion of contracted-out plans, those with a strong bequest motive are free to use their residual pension balances to purchase other annuities which continue paying after their death. Joint life annuities can be purchased which continue paying until the second of two partners dies. Guaranteed annuities are also available which pay out for fixed periods of 5 or 10 years whether or not the annuitant lives. Following an annuitant's death, the remaining payments from a guaranteed annuity may be paid to his or her estate or commuted into a single lump sum payment. By annuitising their pension savings, individuals may also avoid the need, during retirement, to run down their housing wealth or non-pension savings, both of which are fully inheritable.

Inheritability is also facilitated by the option to defer taking an annuity until the age of 75. Until they are annuitised, individual pension savings remain the property of the plan-holder or their estate. In addition, the option to postpone annuitisation permits plan-holders to trade immediate income for the possibility of higher annuity payments in the future. This is because unannuitised funds will continue to earn investment returns and annuity rates are higher for older annuitants. Delaying annuitisation in the hope of higher annuity payments in the future is, however, a risky strategy. Asset values may fall, leaving plan holders with smaller funds to annuitise. Annuity rates may also be reduced if, for example, medical advances improve the survival prospects of older people.

By opting for income drawdown or phased retirement, individuals who defer annuitisation can take an immediate income while investing part of their pension savings for growth. Income drawdown permits individuals below the age of 75 to draw part of their pension savings each year as income – within strict legal limits – with the remaining balance invested for growth. Phased retirement is where different portions (known as segments) of a person's pension savings are annuitised at different times. Unannuitised segments remain invested, but the whole fund must be annuitised by age 75. Both income drawdown and phased retirement leave unannuitised funds available for inheritance and provide scope for efficient retirement income planning. The extra complexity and risk inherent in these products means, however, that they are only suitable for annuitants with large terminal funds, typically £100,000 plus.

The range of annuity products available and the different retirement income options open to annuitants suggest that perceptions of a lack of flexibility in the compulsory annuitisation regime are largely unfounded. A more significant problem may be the complexity of the regime. With so many annuity products to choose from, and a variety of different ways in which they can be combined, most individuals will require advice in selecting an optimum annuitisation strategy. Few annuitants have the necessary financial expertise to do this for themselves. Yet, as some commentators (Orszag 2000, Stark and Curry 2002) have noted, the availability of specialist annuity advice is currently rather limited. Although help is available from commercial annuity advisors, large numbers of annuitants may be unaware that they need advice. Future reform of the compulsory annuitisation regime might, therefore, usefully focus on the need to get advice to those who do not actively seek it.

2.6 THE MAXWELL AFFAIR

On 14 February 1992, the pension schemes of Mirror Group Newspapers (MGN) and Maxwell Communications Corporation (MCC) were wound-up and their members transferred to SERPS. This followed an investigation by the Serious Fraud Office (SFO), begun in December 1991, into how Robert Maxwell, the executive chairman of these businesses, had managed to lose more than £400 million of MGN and MCC pension scheme assets. The SFO's investigation revealed Maxwell's business empire to be riddled with fraud, corruption and incompetence. At the time of Maxwell's mysterious death at sea, in November 1991, the MGN and MCC pension funds were owed, respectively, £350 and £65 million. The schemes were, in fact, insolvent, even though the documentation they and their sponsoring employers submitted to the supervisory authorities implied that they were financially sound (Occupational Pensions Board 1997).

The MGN and MCC pension schemes were plunged into insolvency as a result of a series of share loans they made to two of Maxwell's private companies, Headington Investments and Robert Maxwell Group. These loans were secured against collateral of between 125 and 150 per cent of the value of the borrowed shares (Blake 1992). Along with other Maxwell companies, however, Headington Investments and Robert Maxwell Group were in serious financial difficulty. It became clear after his death that, during the six months before he died, Maxwell had sold much of the collateral used to secure the share loans in a fruitless attempt to stave off the collapse of his private business empire. The upshot was that when Headington Investments and Robert Maxwell Group were taken into administrative receivership, in December 1991, the MGN and MCC schemes, both of which had once been in financial surplus, were no longer able to meet their liabilities to pensioners.

The government of the day responded to the Maxwell affair by establishing the Pension Law Review Committee, in June 1993. The remit of the Committee, which was chaired by Professor Roy Goode (and thus became known as the Goode Committee) was to make recommendations on ways to improve the security of pension fund assets. The Committee deliberated for more than a year, taking evidence from a wide range of interested organisations, including the now defunct Occupational Pensions Board (OPB). The OPB had advised governments on regulatory matters relating to occupational schemes since 1973. It was also responsible for ensuring that schemes complied with the rules in respect of contracting out and the provision of the GMP.

In its evidence to the Goode Committee, the OPB drew attention to what it regarded as important weaknesses in the existing arrangements for protecting the interests of occupational pension scheme members. These included a lack of communication between scheme members and administrators, the poor quality of the information that was provided to members, and the absence of relevant skills among trustees, as well as a lack of clarity regarding their role and responsibilities. The OPB also noted the lack of any mechanism for compensating victims of pension scheme fraud, misappropriation or negligence. It was also concerned about the way regulatory responsibility was split between a number of different agencies and the lack of sanctions, where, as in the Maxwell case, schemes are guilty of misreporting.

As well as arguing for the establishment of a mechanism for compensating victims of pension scheme crime, and financial penalties for misreporting, the OPB suggested a number of other ways to improve matters. It recommended that there should be just one regulator for occupational pensions. It also suggested that trustee boards would be improved by the appointment of employee trustees, and that, as a matter of good practice, trustees should receive adequate training for the job. The Board also suggested 'that solvency requirements and strict financial supervision should apply to all schemes' (Occupational Pensions Board 1997). In addition, it argued for the creation of an effective mechanism for resolving disputes between scheme members, trustees and employers.

The report of the Goode Committee, which was published in September 1993, endorsed many of the ideas suggested by the OPB. Like the OPB, the Committee believed that responsibility for regulating occupational pension schemes should be concentrated in a single authority. What is more, this authority should routinely scrutinise schemes' financial statements. The Committee also recommended measures to improve the flow of information, including the appointment of scheme members to Boards of Trustees. Although many schemes already had member trustees, this was not a legal requirement (Davis 1995). Other recommendations included the establishment of a compensation scheme covering up to 90 per cent of losses arising from fraud or theft, and the introduction of a minimum funding rule. In a subsequent White Paper entitled 'Security Equality and Choice, the Future for Pensions', the government accepted the Goode Committee's recommendations, which, with some modification, were incorporated in the 1995 Pensions Act.

The Act, which came into force in April 1997, swept away the old system of regulation. The OPB was abolished and replaced by the Occupational Pensions Regulatory Authority (OPRA). The OPRA comprises 7 government-appointed members, supported by a staff of around 200. It has very substantial powers – it can, for example, appoint and remove trustees, fine employers and trustees, inspect premises and require schemes to be wound up. As Davis (2001) observes, however, in one respect the Authority's powers are somewhat weaker than those proposed by the Goode Committee, in that it relies on whistle-blowers rather than the routine inspection of scheme financial statements to discover misdemeanours.

As well as providing guarantees for members' funds and extending the role of the Pensions Ombudsman, the Pensions Act made the appointment of member-nominated trustees (MNts) mandatory. It also made trustees subject to financial penalties if they fail to exercise their duties and responsibilities properly. The Act made trustees explicitly responsible for setting schemes' investment principles, ensuring that the rules on self-investment are adhered to and appointing auditors and actuaries. The Act's most far-reaching provisions, however – at least in terms of their impact on the behaviour of schemes and sponsoring companies – were those relating to the indexation of benefits and solvency rules.

The 1995 Act scrapped the GMP. In its place, it introduced the requirement for schemes to increase pension benefits annually in line with inflation, up to a maximum of 5 per cent. In addition, the solvency rules contained in the Act took the form of a minimum funding requirement (MFR). This requires that schemes have sufficient assets such that if they were to be wound up, pensioners' benefits could be secured through the purchase of annuities, and non-pensioners would be able to receive an actuarially fair transfer value for their accrued pension rights. For practical purposes, a 10 per cent deficit is permitted, with schemes having five years in which to return to full solvency. Schemes with deficits greater than 10 per cent must return to 90 per cent solvency within one year.

2.7 THE PERILS OF SELF-INVESTMENT

The losses experienced by the MGN and MCC pension funds arising from the collapse of Robert Maxwell's business empire were not just the result of bad loans. They were due, in part, to high levels of self-investment, which ensured that the value of these funds was heavily dependent upon the success of the Maxwell group of companies. This was a clear breach of UK trust law, which lays a duty on pension fund trustees to avoid exposing scheme beneficiaries to undue risk. The trustee and investment manager of the MGN and MCC funds was Bishopsgate Investment Management (BIM), and the directors of BIM included Robert Maxwell and his sons Kevin and Ian. In 1999, however, Kevin and Ian Maxwell were cleared in court of any wrongdoing.

Investment by a pension fund in the shares of its sponsoring employer is not, in itself, a bad thing. Indeed, where the sponsor is a blue chip company a degree of self-investment may well be desirable. It may also be desirable where the sponsor's shares offer above average investment returns. As the Maxwell affair demonstrated, though, imprudent self-investment makes workers particularly vulnerable to the bankruptcy of the sponsor. When Robert Maxwell took control of MGN's pension fund, in 1985, its investments were mainly in the shares of UK blue chip companies. Yet, as Howells and Bain (1998) observe, by April 1990 more than half of the twenty largest investments in the fund's portfolio were in the shares of companies with which Maxwell had a connection, or in his own private companies. The value of these investments was wiped out when MGN and the other Maxwell companies folded, creating a massive loss for

MGN's pension fund. Consequently, MGN employees lost their pension savings as well as their livelihoods.

The perils of self-investment were illustrated more recently with the collapse of the Houston-based energy firm Enron, which filed for bankruptcy in December 2001. In the 1980s Enron had been little more than a pipeline business supplying natural gas. By the late 1990s, however, it had grown to become America's largest and most aggressive energy-trading company. Its demise was not due to adverse business conditions or even bad luck. It was, instead, the result of incompetence, corrupt business practices and financial chicanery. To cover up mounting losses arising from a series of bungled forays into various sectors of the wholesale energy market, Enron had engaged in some of the most sophisticated forms of creative accounting. As its share price soared, investors were unaware that bogus profits were being reported in order to hide a mountain of debt. In the autumn of 2001, however, the company's shares plummeted after rumours that all was not well at Enron began to circulate. In November 2001 Enron's shares were trading at around $10, compared with nearly $50 in July.

The collapse in Enron's share price had a devastating impact on the company's $2 billion 401(k) pension plan. Enron's 21,000 workers had around 60 per cent of their 401(k) investments in the company's own shares. There were two reasons for this very high level of self-investment. Rather than contributing to its employee's 401(k) accounts with cash, Enron's contributions were paid in company shares. This allowed Enron to benefit from tax relief on its pension contributions without having to part with any cash. In addition, Enron employees could choose from a variety of investment options. Many chose to hold part of their 401(k) accounts in Enron shares. By doing so, they made themselves doubly vulnerable to a fall in the company's share price.

In some respects the situation at Enron was exceptional. Enron employees had the misfortune to work for an organisation which was managed by some corrupt and unscrupulous individuals. They were also prohibited by the company from selling their 401(k) holdings of Enron shares if they were below the age of 50. Moreover, while the share price was falling, in October and November 2001, Enron was in the middle of switching its 401(k) pension plan's administrator. Consequently, even employees over the age of 50 were unable to liquidate their holdings of Enron shares before they became worthless. By contrast, some of Enron's top executives got rich by selling shares worth millions of dollars. Enron was far from exceptional, though, in the high level of self-investment in its 401(k) pension plan.

Many US corporations make contributions to their employees' 401(k) accounts in the form of their own company shares. These companies typically have around one-third of their 401(k) plans self-invested. This compares with about 19 per cent for all 401(k) plans. While a high level of self-investment is contrary to the principles of prudent diversification, it is perfectly legal. Although US pensions regulation imposes a 10 per cent limit on self-investment, the restriction only applies to defined benefit schemes. The 401(k) plans of some of America's largest and most venerable companies – members of the Fortune 500, with thousands of employees – have self-investment levels above 60 per cent. For example, in 2002, Coca-Cola and General Electric had about 75 per cent of their 401(k) plans invested in their own shares. The equivalent figure for Procter & Gamble was just under 95 per cent.

The official response to the Enron affair was swift. Less than 24 hours after the US Justice Department announced that it had launched a criminal investigation into the company's collapse, President Bush instructed his Treasury Secretary, Paul O'Neill, to conduct a review of pension law. An obvious option open to the authorities is to place limits on self-investment in 401(k) plans similar to those that apply to DB schemes. Such a move would almost certainly be opposed by corporate America, since it would deprive companies of a valuable tax break. Ordinary Americans might also object. Investing heavily in their employer's stock, through their 401(k) accounts, has allowed large numbers of workers with modest incomes to enjoy an affluent retirement.

Enron was not the only firm to restrict its employees' ability to sell their 401(k) holdings of company shares. Even where there is no requirement for workers below a certain age to hold onto their company stock, many firms place a 10-year moratorium on company share disposals. President Bush's own reform proposals, announced in February 2002, included giving all contributors to 401(k) plans the right to sell their holdings of company stock three years after acquiring them. Given that Enron's share price collapsed within the space of a few months, even with the right to sell company shares bought three years earlier, Enron's employees would still have incurred massive losses. Two Democratic senators, Barbara Boxer and Jon Corzine, introduced a bill, also in February 2002, that would allow workers to sell their 401(k) company share holdings after just three months. Other reform proposals involve a mandatory requirement for employers to educate their workers about the risks of undiversified share holdings when they first join a 401(k) plan, with annual reminders thereafter. Diamond (2002), however, suggests that the potential for worker education to improve investment decisions may be rather limited.

2.8 SOLVENCY, ACCOUNTING AND OCCUPATIONAL SCHEME CLOSURES

Before April 1997, when the 1995 Pensions Act came into force, responsibility for the solvency of UK DB occupational schemes lay with trustees, who had a duty of care to ensure that schemes were adequately funded.

There was, however, no standard method of calculating funding (Davis, 2001). Although sponsors had a legal duty to make good scheme deficits, they were under no obligation to report these in their company accounts. The only other statutory requirement in respect of solvency related to the GMP. Schemes were required to hold sufficient assets to meet their contracted-out benefit obligations. The changes in UK pension law arising from the Maxwell affair closely mirrored reforms introduced in the United States more than 20 years earlier.

In 1974, the US Congress passed the Employee Retirement Income Security Act (ERISA). As well as introducing IRAs and tightening the rules on vesting, ERISA sought to improve the security of employer-provided DB schemes by compelling their sponsors to meet strict new funding requirements. This followed the collapse of several companies with underfunded pension schemes, where pensioners had lost everything. The effect of ERISA and subsequent legislation was to force employers to ensure that their DB schemes were capable of meeting their current obligations to members in full in the event of an immediate wind-up. What is more, sponsors with scheme deficits are required by US Accounting Standard FAS 87 – introduced in December 1985 – to report the shortfall in their company accounts.

ERISA also created the Pension Benefit Guarantee Corporation (PBGC) to provide partial benefit protection for members of occupational DB schemes where the employer becomes bankrupt. The PBGC is financed from premiums paid by the companies whose schemes it insures and from investment returns on these premiums. In 2002, it guaranteed the pension payments of those retiring at age 65 up to a maximum of nearly $43,000. To encourage adequate funding of pension benefits, and to limit the potential for deliberate under-funding, the premiums charged by the PBGC are lower for sponsors with well-funded schemes – less than a third of those charged to firms with the largest deficits.

As noted in Section 2.6, the Pensions Act of 1995 established the MFR as the standard measure of solvency for UK DB occupational pension schemes. A requirement for sponsors to provide information about the solvency of their schemes in their company accounts was also introduced when, in November 2000, the Accounting Standards Board (ASB) issued Financial Reporting Standard 17: Pension Benefits, known as FRS 17 for short. Although the 1995 legislation established compensation arrangements for victims of pension fraud, it stopped short of introducing PBGC-style protection for the pension benefits of bankrupt firms. The question of whether Britain needs its own version of the PBGC is considered in Section 2.9 below.

The government of the day went ahead with the decision to introduce the MFR despite objections from employers, pension fund managers and academics. Opponents of the MFR argued that it was too costly and would, in any case, fail to deliver improved security for members of occupational pension schemes. As Section 1.4 shows, occupational pension funds have traditionally invested heavily in equities. Yet, by requiring schemes to insure that the value of their assets was always sufficient to meet their obligations to members, the MFR would force fund managers to allocate a greater proportion of their scheme's investments to less volatile, but lower-yielding, bonds. To make up for lower returns, employers would find it necessary to make larger payments to their pension schemes. The increase in costs would be greatest for large firms with mature schemes. Many of these firms could be expected to close their DB schemes to new members – and possibly existing members – in order to cut costs.

There is some evidence that the introduction of the MFR did indeed lead pension fund managers to increase the proportion of bonds in their schemes' investment portfolios. Data from the WM Company (cited in Davis 2001) show that in 1998, the year after the MFR came into force, bonds accounted for 19 per cent of pension fund assets, and equities 72 per cent. In 1995 the respective proportions were 14 per cent and 76 per cent. As Davis (2001) points out, though, the distorting effect of the MFR on pension scheme investments should not be overstated. Other factors were also leading fund managers to invest more in bonds. For example, the abolition of dividend tax credits for pension schemes, in 1997, increased the relative attractiveness of bonds by reducing the returns from equity investments. Moreover, as schemes matured they would have increased their holdings of bonds so as to match increasing short term liabilities with a more stable income stream.

Although a trend for firms to close their defined benefit schemes to new employees and provide them with money purchase plans instead was already established by the mid-1990s, the pace of scheme closures accelerated following the introduction of the MFR. By 2001, the rate of scheme closures had risen to nearly one a week. Whilst companies cited higher costs associated with the MFR, most blamed the decision to close their DB schemes on the need to avoid potential problems arising from compliance with FRS 17. While the new accounting standard was scheduled for full implementation in company accounts for periods ending on or after 22 June 2003, the ASB was keen to encourage earlier adoption where possible.

Employers worried about FRS 17 because it would radically change the way they account for DB pension costs when it replaced the existing accounting rules contained in Statement of Standard Accounting Practice (SSAP) 24. SSAP 24 requires firms to treat DB pension contributions as a charge in the administrative expenses sections of their profit and loss accounts. Since scheme deficits necessitate firms increasing their annual contributions, they show up in the accounts as higher administrative expenses. The reverse is true in the case of surpluses, because contribution holidays taken to reduce a surplus lead to lower administrative expenses.

FRS 17, however, forces firms to record the funding level of their pension schemes as a balance-sheet item. A surplus must be listed as an asset and a deficit as a liability.

Companies were concerned about the additional administrative costs associated with FRS 17 compliance. Unlike SSAP 24, which required schemes to be actuarially valued on a triennial basis, FRS 17 would necessitate annual valuations. Even more worrying, though, was the effect the valuation formula would have on company balance sheets. Although valuations carried out under SSAP 24 compare a scheme's liabilities with the value of its assets, asset prices can be averaged over a number of years to take account of fluctuations in their market price. FRS 17 permits no such smoothing. Assets are valued on their current market price. Because equity values fluctuate over time, and equities represent the bulk of defined benefit scheme assets, FRS 17 will have the effect of introducing a highly volatile item onto company balance sheets.

To minimise the balance-sheet volatility created for sponsors of DB schemes by FRS 17, pension funds would have an incentive to switch a substantial portion of their investments from equities to bonds. This is because, in order to calculate the current value of pension liabilities that have to be met in the future, FRS 17 demands that the nominal cost of these long-term liabilities be discounted by the rate of return on high quality corporate bonds. The equivalent discount rate under SSAP 24 was the return on equities. At a little above the return on risk-free gilt-edged securities, the return on high quality corporate bonds has historically been significantly lower than the return on equities. Thus, instead of enhancing pension scheme solvency, which depends on investment returns rather than the market price of scheme assets, FRS 17 would raise the cost of DB schemes for employers and increase the risk of insolvencies by encouraging funds to invest in low-yielding assets.

In his budget speech of 2001, the Chancellor of the Exchequer, Gordon Brown, announced that he was accepting in full the recommendations of the Myners Committee and would be scrapping the MFR. The Myners Committee had been set up a year earlier by Gordon Brown to carry out a detailed review of institutional investment. At the time, the Chancellor had been concerned that small companies were being starved of much needed funds by a risk-averse investment management industry which failed to invest enough in private equities, preferring instead the shares of publicly quoted companies. When it published its report, however, the Committee – chaired by Paul Myners, the Chairman of Gartmore Investment Management – had little to say about private equity investment.

Myners was highly critical of the MFR. In particular, he argued that for many funds, future investment returns and the investment strategy of fund managers were more important for a scheme's ability to meet its obligations than the current ratio of assets to liabilities. He recommended that the one-size-fits-all MFR be abolished and replaced with long-term, scheme-specific funding standards. This should be backed up by greater transparency. The investment strategies of individual funds should be determined by trustees, based on professional advice, and there should be full disclosure of the value and distribution of scheme assets. In addition, Myners recommended that schemes should be obliged to justify their investment strategies by providing information about the assumed level of investment returns and future contributions. They should also be required to state clearly their expectations about future asset values.

The abolition of the MFR and its replacement with scheme-specific funding standards could not be effected immediately. It required both primary and secondary legislation. Interim measures were therefore introduced to ease the burden that the MFR imposes on schemes until the necessary legislation could be passed. These measures included an extension, until 31 December 2004, of the transitional period (originally set to end on 5 April 2002), after which full MFR compliance was mandatory for all schemes. The deficit correction periods were also extended, to allow firms with under-funded schemes more time to return them to full MFR solvency. Following the announcement that the MFR was to be scrapped, the ASB announced, in July 2002, that it was extending the deadline for firms to comply with FRS 17 by a year. While the ASB said that it was delaying implementation prior to the publication of an international accounting standard for sponsors of DB pension schemes, the possibility must exist that FRS 17, like the MFR, will ultimately be abandoned altogether.

2.9 A PENSION BENEFIT GUARANTEE CORPORATION FOR THE UK

As well as failing to protect workers' pension rights when a solvent firm winds up its defined benefit scheme, the current regulatory regime also fails past and present employees of insolvent firms. This is something that the 4,000 employees and former workers of Allied Steel and Wire discovered when their company went into receivership in July 2002. There were insufficient funds in the company's two DB schemes to meet pension obligations in full. Consequently, the firm's employees were expected to receive substantially less than the full value of their accrued pension rights, despite one of the schemes being more than 100 per cent funded on an MFR basis. In situations like this older workers are hit hardest, since they have less time in the labour market than their younger colleagues in which to make up their pension shortfalls through additional saving.

There are two reasons why the current regulatory regime fails to provide complete security for participants of DB schemes when their employer goes bankrupt. The first relates to the 'prioritisation' rules. The second derives from the formula used to calculate solvency levels under the MFR. Under the 1995 Pensions Act, existing pensioners are given a prior claim on the assets of schemes where the sponsoring firm is insolvent. The firm's current employees must share what's left over after existing pensioners' rights have been bought out in full. This may be very little. The MFR undervalues schemes' liabilities by assuming more generous annuity rates than those actually available in the market. Thus schemes which appear to be secure on an MFR basis can turn out to be substantially under-funded.

Had Allied Steel and Wire been an American company, its employees would have had their accrued pension rights protected by the PBGC. In March 2002, for example, the PBGC announced that it was taking over pension payments for 82,000 members of three under-funded pension schemes sponsored by the bankrupt US steel maker LTV. The lack of any similar protection for workers in the UK begs the question whether Britain should have its own version of the PBGC. Sweden and Germany both have arrangements for insuring workers' pension benefits. In Sweden, schemes pay premiums worth 0.2 per cent of their pension liabilities to a benefit insurance scheme. In Germany, workers' pension benefit guarantees are paid for by their employers.

In fact, a benefit insurance scheme may not be the best way to protect workers' occupational pension rights because it can give rise to moral hazard. Moral hazard can occur where an insured party is fully protected and so has a diminished incentive to avoid risk. If, for example, someone has the contents of their home fully insured against theft, they may become less diligent about closing and locking doors and windows when they go out. They know that the cost of replacing their possessions, if stolen, will be met by their insurer. Where workers' pension benefits are subject to 100 per cent insurance, fund managers may be tempted to make excessively risky investments. In so doing, they may actually lose members' funds. This situation is especially likely where fund managers' remuneration is linked to investment returns.

That moral hazard is more than just a theoretical possibility was amply demonstrated by the collapse of numerous US savings and loan institutions in the late 1980s (Hall 1991). Following the introduction of a 100 per cent deposit insurance scheme, managers of savings and loan institutions – the equivalent of British building societies – began to make increasingly risky investments. Knowing their savings to be protected, depositors had no incentive to monitor what was going on and insist that managers make more prudent investments. When these investments went bad, dozens of savings and loan institutions folded. To prevent moral hazard, it is necessary to force insured parties to bear some risk. The PBGC does this by placing a limit on the value of the benefits it insures. This gives members of insured schemes an incentive to make sure that their fund managers do not take excessive risks, since they are not fully covered against the loss of their funds. The reduction in moral hazard is, therefore, bought at the cost of less than full benefit protection.

Pension benefit insurance may also fail to protect scheme members where the cost of providing it is high. Firms may elect to close their DB schemes, as many US companies did after the PBGC was set up. By providing workers with money purchase plans instead, US firms were able to avoid paying benefit insurance premiums to the PBGC. Moreover, high insurance premiums could themselves contribute to corporate bankruptcies. The obligation to meet their benefit insurance payments could be the final straw for financially distressed companies. This is likely to be a particularly serious problem for large firms in depressed or declining industries. Yet, as the PBGC's own experience shows, high premiums may be needed if a benefit insurance scheme is to be self-financing.

In 1974, the PBGC believed it could cover its costs by charging employers an annual premium of $1 per worker. Premiums were accordingly set at this level. Claims on the Corporation were, however, much higher than anticipated, following the collapse of several firms with large pension scheme deficits, and defaults on benefit payments by schemes which had been deliberately under-funded. Consequently, the PBGC was itself in financial deficit for the first 20 years of its existence. By the mid-1980s, it was estimated that annual premiums of $50 per worker were needed for the PBGC to cover its costs (Blake 1992). In 1987 the funding rules for US DB schemes were tightened, yet by late 1991 the PBGC had an estimated deficit of $2.5 bn (Davis 1995). In November 2003, Steve Kandarian, the head of the PBGC, announced that by July that year the corporation's deficit had risen to $5.7 billion (US).

To keep pension guarantee premiums low in Germany, only vested benefits are insured. Since vesting periods are long in Germany, this means that the pension benefits of large numbers of workers are, in fact, uninsured.

In July 2003, the British government announced its intention to establish a PBGC-style pension protection fund (PPF) for the UK. The PPF, which will not come into operation until April 2005 at the earliest, will cover 90 per cent of DB scheme members' pension rights, up to a maximum of about £50,000 per annum. Like America's PBGC, the PPF will be self-financing. To this end, it will impose a dual levy on the schemes it protects. All schemes will pay a flat-rate levy plus a risk-related levy, such that the largest amounts will be paid by the least well-funded schemes. As well as providing an incentive for poorly-funded schemes to improve their financial position, the risk-related levy is intended to ensure that 'sound schemes' do not end up subsidising vulnerable schemes.

Because the PPF will not fully insure workers' DB pension rights, the risk of moral hazard arising will be somewhat lower than it is with the PGBC. There is still the possibility, though, that, as in America, British firms might choose to wind up their DB schemes in preference to paying the PPF levy. Thus, far from protecting DB schemes, the PPF could play a significant role in hastening their demise. On the same day that the government announced the setting up of the PPF, regulations were introduced, with immediate effect, which place a legal obligation on employers who voluntarily wind up their DB schemes to make up any funding shortfall prior to winding up. These regulations will prevent a repeat of the scandalous situation where workers with a year or two to go before retirement see the pension contributions they have made for decades go to secure the pensions of those ahead in the prioritisation queue, leaving them with little or nothing.

The potential must exist for the PPF to suffer similar financing difficulties to those recently experienced by the PBGC. If, as a result of its introduction, the number of DB schemes is greatly reduced by a spate of voluntary wind-ups, there may be fewer than anticipated paying the PPF levy. Moreover, calls on the PPF will be precipitated by sponsor insolvencies. These can, but rarely do, occur in isolation. The annual number of corporate bankruptcies tends to rise during a recession and fall during a boom. The cyclical nature of corporate bankruptcies suggests that calls on the PPF are likely to come in clusters rather than one at a time.

2.10 THE PERSONAL PENSIONS MIS-SELLING SCANDAL

The mis-selling of personal pension plans in Britain in the late 1980s and early 1990s was a scandal of monumental proportions. It affected more than a million people, took eight years to clear up, and severely dented the reputation of the financial services industry. Massive fines were imposed on some of Britain's most respected insurance companies, and the pensions industry was forced to spend billions of pounds compensating the victims of mis-selling. At the heart of the scandal were two essential ingredients, ignorance and greed; ignorance on the part of the purchasers of these products and greed on the part of those who sold them.

Until 1988, the UK's supplementary pension arrangements had been characterised by an absence of choice. Employees either made contributions to SERPS, or they contributed to a contracted-out occupational pension scheme, if their employer provided one. Employers usually made membership of their company schemes a condition of employment. Thus, most people who opted out of SERPS did so at their employer's behest. Since contracted-out schemes provided as good, or better, pension benefits than SERPS, workers had little cause to complain. The government, on the other hand, regarded compulsory membership of occupational schemes as an unwarranted restraint on individuals' freedom. In 1988, the introduction of PPPs was accompanied by a change in the law, making membership of company schemes voluntary. Employees could now choose for themselves whether to contribute to SERPS, their employer's scheme, or a personal pension plan.

With three schemes to choose from, each having advantages and disadvantages which differed according to individuals' circumstances, making the right choice was no easy matter. It required a detailed knowledge of how the different schemes worked – something that most people could not be expected to possess. It came as no surprise, then, that people looked to the pensions industry itself for advice. They were unaware, however, that those giving advice were not unbiased. The salaries received by advisors usually depended on the commissions they earned on each PPP they sold, and therefore advisors had a financial interest in promoting PPPs over other forms of supplementary pension provision. By the time anyone noticed what was going on, tens of thousands of people had been wrongly persuaded to leave an employers scheme – or not to join one – and contribute instead to a PPP. Those affected included police officers, firefighters, teachers, nurses and miners.

By the early 1990s, the first cases of pensions mis-selling were beginning to come to light. In its February 1992 bulletin, LAUTRO announced that the staff of an un-named insurance company were systematically transferring workers from an attractive occupational scheme into PPPs. A year later, the Securities and Investments Board (SIB) commissioned the accountancy firm KPMG to look into the scale of the problem. KPMG examined a random sample of 735 transfers from occupational schemes, which had taken place between 1991 and 1993. Their findings suggested that over 90 per cent of transfers could have been the result of mis-selling. The SIB responded by setting up a steering group of regulatory chiefs to advise it on how to clean up the pensions industry and establish the criteria for compensating those who had been mis-sold PPPs.

In 1994, the SIB instructed insurance companies to carry out a review of their sales of PPPs between 29 April 1988 and 30 June 1994, and to make good any losses arising from mis-selling. Although up to a million people were thought to have been mis-sold a PPP, the insurance companies were instructed to deal with around 700,000 urgent cases first. These 'priority' cases involved people who, by the time the review began, had already retired or were close to retirement. Less urgent cases, mainly involving people in their thirties and forties, were to be filed for attention at a later date. The pensions review took eight years to complete, at a cost of some 13.5 billion pounds to insurers and pensions advisors.

Originally, the intention of the review was to identify cases of mis-selling and to reinstate those affected in the occupational schemes they had left, without loss of benefits. In the vast majority of cases, however, this proved impossible. Some schemes had been wound up. Others had suspended the right to buy back missing years. For most people, redress took the form of a cash top-up to their PPP. The value of these top-ups was based upon a person's age at the time he or she transferred to a PPP, and upon actuarial assumptions about trends in life expectancy and investment returns. By December 2000, more than 98 per cent of priority cases had been reviewed. Nearly 3.6 billion pounds had been paid out in compensation to 406,000 people – an average of £8,800 each. Phase two, the review of younger peoples' pensions, began in January 1999.

The pensions review was officially concluded in June 2001. This, however, may not be the end of the PPP mis-selling story. In August 2001 the Consumers' Association called for the re-opening of compensation cases where recent stock market falls were likely to result in short-falls. Two years of falling equity values meant that, if the compensation payments to PPPs were to leave the victims of mis-selling no worse off than they would otherwise have been, future investment returns would have to rise to unrealistic levels. For its part, the Treasury said it was keeping an eye on the situation, but had no plans to re-open the compensation issue.

2.11 THE EQUITABLE LIFE FIASCO

As the process of identifying and compensating the victims of personal pension mis-selling was drawing to a close, the UK pensions industry was rocked by another scandal. This time, though, only one company, the Equitable Life Assurance Society, was involved. Established in 1762, Equitable Life was the world's oldest mutually-owned life insurer. It had an impeccable reputation for probity and astute financial management, yet for decades Equitable Life had been flouting some of the most basic principles of insurance. By the mid-1990s, the Society had got itself into the position of being unable to honour pension promises made to hundreds of thousands of policyholders since the late 1950s.

In 1957, Equitable Life began selling with-profits life assurance policies offering guaranteed annuity rates (GARs) on single life fixed annuities. When they retired, holders of these policies had the option to purchase an annuity from Equitable Life at either the GAR or the current market rate. Since market annuity rates are variable, rising and falling in line with bond interest rates, GAR policyholders were provided with a degree of protection against down-side risk. In effect, the variability of annuity rates was limited to rates above the GAR. These policies proved extremely popular; between 1957 and 1988, Equitable Life sold around 90,000.

In selling GAR policies, Equitable Life took on a combination of interest rate and mortality risk. In 1957 the GARs it offered were low relative to market annuity rates. As long as market rates remained above its GARs, the funds from maturing policies could be annuitised at no cost to the Society. There was always the risk, however, that falling interest rates and/or increases in average life expectancy might drive market annuity rates down. If market rates were to fall below its guaranteed rates, the income from the bonds used to back Equitable's annuities would be insufficient to cover annuity payments. In this case, honouring its annuity rate guarantees would be costly for the Society. Moreover, the lower the market rate compared with the rates Equitable Life guaranteed to pay, the more expensive its GARS would become.

Other insurers were also selling GAR policies. The practice among these insurers was to hedge their exposure to interest rate and mortality risk by re-insuring their GAR policies and setting up contingency reserves. Some insurers made arrangements for buying out their GAR commitments, or placed limits on the value of funds covered by these guarantees. By contrast, and contrary to the most fundamental principles of insurance, Equitable Life did not hedge its GAR exposure. The Society was, in effect, gambling on market annuity rates remaining above its GARs long into the future. Although the Society stopped selling GAR policies in 1988, it would remain exposed to interest rate and mortality risk well into the twenty-first century.

By the early 1990s, annuity market conditions were very different from those prevailing in the late 1950s. A combination of falling interest rates and increasing life expectancy was steadily driving down market annuity rates. In October 1993, market rates fell below those Equitable Life had guaranteed to pay its GAR policyholders – typically 12.5 per cent. The society realised immediately that it faced a potential disaster. In December 1993 it moved to neutralise its annuity guarantees through the introduction of a differential final bonus. Since part of a policyholder's funds at maturity came from a terminal bonus, Equitable Life would pay reduced bonuses to individuals who exercised their GAR rights rather than taking the lower market annuity rate. GARs would be paid, but on smaller funds. This way, GAR policyholders would receive the same income they would have got from an annuity purchased at market rates.

It took some time for GAR policyholders to realise the significance of Equitable Life's new approach to final bonuses. Meanwhile, market annuity rates continued to fall. By 1998, they were more than 20 per cent below Equitable Life's guaranteed rates. The majority of GAR policyholders only became aware of what was happening when Equitable Life became the subject of hostile coverage in the press following the publication of a report, 'The Good, the Bad and the Ugly', by Stuart Bayliss, Director of the independent consultancy 'The Annuity Bureau'. A campaign group was formed to lobby on behalf of GAR policyholders. It alleged breach of contract and accused Equitable Life's board of abusing its powers of discretion in the apportioning of final bonuses. The Society responded by seeking a ruling in the High Court on the legality of its final bonus policy.

In September 1999, the High Court ruled in Equitable Life's favour. Its GAR policyholders immediately lodged an appeal and, in January 2000, the Appeal Court overturned the earlier High Court ruling. By this time market annuity rates had fallen further. Honouring its GAR obligations would now cost Equitable Life around £1.5 billion. Now it was the Society's turn to appeal. On 20 July 2000, though, the House of Lords found Equitable Life's treatment of GAR policyholders to be unfair and dismissed its appeal. With no further legal channels open to it, Equitable Life was now in deep trouble. External financing to plug the hole in its with-profits fund had been secured, but this was conditional on Equitable Life receiving a favourable judgement in the House of Lords. Consequently, the only source of funds available to honour the Society's GAR commitments was the with-profits fund itself.

Only a minority of Equitable Life's with-profits policyholders had GAR policies. The Society had also sold hundreds of thousands of policies that did not contain annuity rate guarantees. As a result of the House of Lords ruling, it now faced the prospect of being sued for mis-selling by these non-GAR policyholders. In an attempt to raise the funds it needed to honour its GAR obligations, Equitable Life began a desperate search for a buyer. It also increased the proportion of its with-profits fund invested in bonds. While a move away from equities into bonds was the right thing to do for its GAR policyholders, it was wholly inappropriate for those with non-GAR policies, and gave additional weight to any action they might bring for mis-selling.

There were several aspects to Equitable Life's mis-selling of non-GAR policies. All involved a departure from basic insurance and investment principles. Unlike other insurers who sold GAR policies, Equitable Life did not separate the funds of its GAR and non-GAR policyholders. Instead, both groups were invested in the same with-profits fund. It was impossible, therefore, to meet the portfolio needs of both investor groups simultaneously. A key axiom of insurance is that different asset types are appropriate for matching different forms of risk. For guaranteed investments like GARs, an appropriate portfolio allocation would be one heavily weighted in favour of bonds. Where no guarantees exist, as with non-GAR policies, a portfolio dominated by higher-yielding, but riskier, equities is appropriate.

A fundamental principle of pooled investments is that expected returns should be the same for all investors. Yet the potential for market annuity rates to fall below those guaranteed by Equitable Life meant that, with a common fund without re-insurance or reserves, returns to non-GAR policyholders could be reduced because of the Society's obligation to meet the claims of investors holding GARs. Equitable Life did not differentiate between its policyholders. GAR and Non-GAR policyholders paid the same premiums. Non-GAR policyholders were, in effect, insuring the guarantees of those holding GAR policies free of charge. Not only were those who bought non-GAR policies not made aware of the risks they were taking on, they also received no offsetting compensation. Consequently, Equitable Life was in breach of two key principles of insurance: that buyers of insurance should pay premiums which reflect the risks covered, and that providers of insurance should be fully compensated for the risks they bear.

While it searched for a buyer, Equitable Life continued selling non-GAR policies, in spite of the House of Lords ruling. It was not until December 2000 that, with no sale agreed, the with-profits fund was closed to new entrants. In February 2001, the bulk of Equitable Life's non-with-profits business was sold to Halifax plc. In addition to the £150 million paid by the Halifax, the bank agreed to pay a further £250 million – known as the Halifax money – if Equitable Life managed to cap its GAR liabilities and introduce a scheme to preserve the solvency of its with-profits fund by 1 March 2002. To this end, on 6 December 2001, the Board of Equitable Life asked its with-profits fund members to vote on a proposed scheme for compromising its GAR liabilities.

There were two elements to the compromise scheme proposal. First, Equitable Life would buy out its GARs in return for a one-off increase in GAR policyholders' policy values, averaging 17.5 per cent. Second, in return for a 2.5 per cent uplift to their policy values, non-GAR policyholders would give up their right to sue the Society for mis-selling. Before the proposed scheme could be accepted it had to receive a favourable vote from a majority of those voting and representing not less than 75 per cent of voters' combined policy values. It also had to be approved by the High Court. On 11 January 2002, the Scheme received the vote required for its implementation. High Court approval followed, and the scheme was formally registered on 8 February. As a result, Equitable Life became eligible to receive the Halifax money.

The possibility that Equitable Life might be sued for mis-selling was not closed off completely with the adoption of the compromise scheme. Prior to the 11 January vote, large numbers of individuals switched their funds out of Equitable Life, even though the Society imposed a heavy exit penalty. These individuals are not bound by the terms of the scheme and might, in the future, choose to sue. The possibility also exists that a claim for compensation might be pursued against the various authorities which were responsible for regulating Equitable Life's with-profits operations. When the Society began selling GARs, in 1957, it was regulated by the Department for Trade and Industry. Regulatory responsibility was subsequently transferred to the UK Treasury and, in the late 1990s, to the Financial Services Authority.

In the autumn of 2001, the government announced that it was setting up an independent inquiry which would examine the lessons to be learnt from the fiasco at Equitable Life regarding the conduct, administration and regulation of life assurance. Lord Penrose, a Scottish commercial judge, was appointed to head the inquiry. The inquiry published its findings, in an 818-page report, on 8 March 2004. Penrose was highly critical of the regulatory authorities for allowing Equitable Life to jeopardise its policyholders' retirement incomes by failing to hedge its exposure to interest rate and mortality risk. Surprisingly, perhaps, the inquiry's terms of reference made no mention of financial compensation for Equitable

Life policyholders, and the government has also ruled this out, at least for the moment.

It is possible that Equitable Life might eventually reopen its with-profits fund to new members. Before this can happen, though, it must build up a pool of free assets to cover its outstanding GAR obligations so that the fund can take on a higher proportion of equity investments. Subject to Equitable Life meeting certain targets for the sale of Halifax products, the bank has agreed to pay the Society up to £250 million in addition to the original Halifax money. Exit charges on those who transfer out of the with-profits fund represent another source of extra funds. Since the Halifax is currently running Equitable Life on a cost-only basis, earnings from the Society's non-with-profits operations could also be utilised. In addition, in spring 2003, Equitable Life was given leave to pursue a professional negligence claim in the High Court for up to £500 million against its former auditor, Ernst & Young.

2.12 CLOSING THE PENSION SAVINGS GAP

The Green Paper (DWP 2002) sets out the British government's current strategy for ensuring that people have adequate retirement resources in the future. The strategy comprises two elements; longer working lives and increased saving. With life expectancy rising, the government argues that people must either work for longer or save more, or, ideally, do both. Yet, estimates contained in the Green Paper suggest that as many as 3 million people are seriously under-saving for their retirement or are planning to retire too early. In addition, it is suggested that between 5 and 10 million individuals may want to consider saving more and/or working for longer.

Compelling people to work longer or to save more would be fraught with political difficulties. Not surprisingly, then, compulsion has been eschewed in favour of a predominantly voluntarist approach. The Green Paper proposes a strengthening of existing incentives for people to retire later and to save more, as well as the introduction of new ones. In Section 2.2 it was suggested that the approach to retirement contained in the Green Paper is essentially the right one. Here the focus is on the prospects for increased personal saving for retirement.

The system of retirement income provision in the UK is unusual in both its complexity and its reliance on discretionary saving. Compared with many other countries, the state's direct commitment to retirement income provision in Britain is rather modest. Through the combination of a mandatory flat-rate basic pension, compulsory earnings-related state or private supplementary pensions and means-tested benefits, the government guarantees retirees a level of retirement income equal to about a quarter of average earnings. To obtain a post-retirement income in excess of that guaranteed by the state, workers must undertake an amount of additional private pension saving. The tax relief available on private pension contributions (discussed in Section 2.4), coupled with the prospect of minimal retirement incomes for those who make no private pension provision, means that incentives to save for retirement exist in the form of a carrot and a stick.

It has become conventional wisdom among pensions professionals in the UK that, in order to have adequate resources in retirement, individuals should aim to retire with a pension equal to around two-thirds of their pre-retirement earnings. Whether or not the two-thirds rule is a good one, its implications are clear; workers should undertake the level of discretionary saving that will give them a combined public and private pension income equal to 66 per cent of their earnings at retirement. In so far as aggregate saving for retirement is currently below the level required to satisfy the two-thirds rule, Britain can be said to be experiencing a pension savings gap. While the government has been reluctant to put a figure on the size of the savings gap, estimates for the ABI – produced by Oliver Wyman & Company (OWC 2001) – put it at £27 billion per year (see Table 2.12.1).

To close the pension savings gap, Oliver Wyman & Company estimate that savings would need to rise by 54 per cent a year. According to their estimates, more than 50 per cent of working households have a savings shortfall greater than 10 per cent of their annual earnings. They estimate that only those aged over 35, with household incomes greater than £35,000, are likely to be saving enough. Not surprisingly, perhaps, the savings shortfall is estimated to be particularly acute among households with low incomes.

Estimates of the pension savings gap need to be treated with considerable caution. They are only as good as the assumptions on which they are based. The Oliver Wyman estimates, for example, assumed that people work to age 65 and that the return to investments is 7 per cent per annum gross. These were reasonable assumptions to have made. Other equally

Table 2.12.1 Total annual savings gap (£ million) by age and household income

Age (years)	£ per annum						Total
	<9,500	9,500–13,500	13,500–17,500	17,500–25,000	25,000–35,000	>35,000	
Under 25	767	368	393	574	761	1,211	4,074
25–35	1,128	891	999	1,623	1,620	965	7,226
35–45	845	997	1,232	1,631	2,333	0	7,038
45–60	528	1,389	1,130	1,921	3,718	0	8,686
Total	3,268	3,645	3,754	5,749	8,432	2,176	27,024

Source: Association of British Insurers.

reasonable assumptions – e.g. that investment returns are less than 7 per cent and that people retire before age 65 – would have yielded a different estimate. Other things being equal, the lower the assumed rate of return to investments and the earlier people are assumed to retire, the larger will be the estimated savings gap.

Whatever its size, closing the savings gap may turn out to be more difficult than the present government hopes or expects. The level of voluntary saving for retirement may not increase substantially in response to improved incentives. In this case, a future government may take the view that additional compulsory pension contributions are the only way to close the savings gap. There are, in fact, three reasons why the voluntarist approach might fail to deliver substantially higher levels of discretionary pension saving. First, the presence of means testing in the retirement income system acts as a deterrent to saving. Second, the UK's main retirement savings vehicles are not well suited to the needs of some sections of the workforce. Finally, many workers will have been put off from saving for retirement – some permanently – by recent scandals involving UK pension providers.

The purpose of the means-tested component in Britain's state support for pensioners is to provide a safety net – a minimum level of retirement income below which no pensioner should have to sink. The main means-tested retirement benefit is the MIG (minimum income guarantee) which, for a single pensioner in April 2003, stood at £102.10 per week and for couples at £155.80. Pensioners with incomes below the MIG levels are entitled to receive weekly benefit payments equal to the difference between their pension incomes and £102.10 or £155.80. Thus, a 65-year-old single pensioner with only the basic state pension to live on (£77.45 per week in April 2003) would qualify to receive weekly MIG payments of £24.65. Because MIG benefits are withdrawn on a pound-for-pound basis, if the same pensioner had £14 per week of supplementary pension income, his or her MIG entitlement would fall to £10.65.

For low-income workers – those the present government is most keen to see saving more – the MIG constitutes a powerful disincentive to save. The pound-for-pound withdrawal of MIG benefits is, in effect, a 100 per cent tax on the first £24.65 per week of supplementary pension income. Consequently, workers whose savings in 2003 were insufficient to give them a supplementary pension greater than £24.65 would have been no better off than they would have been had they saved nothing. Similarly, to have achieved an income in retirement just £10 per week above the MIG, a pensioner would have had to have saved enough to give him or her £34.65 per week of supplementary pension. A person's eligibility to the MIG is reduced according to a savings taper. This acts as a further disincentive to save. As Curry (2001) notes, pensioners who have saved can end up with lower incomes than those who have not, since a modest amount of capital can remove their entitlement to the MIG altogether.

The government has made it clear that it intends to uprate the MIG each year in line with increases in average nominal earnings. The basic state pension, on the other hand, will continue to be uprated in line with inflation. As a result, the amount of supplementary income subject to the 100 per cent MIG tax will increase over time in line with the rate of growth of average real earnings. As Figure 2.12.1 shows, with an assumed rate of 2 per cent per annum for average real earnings growth, the gap between the basic pension and the MIG will widen from £24.65 in 2003 to £29.85 in 2005, and will reach £90.43 by 2020. By gradually increasing the amount of supplementary income people will need in order to make saving worthwhile, the effect of the widening gap between the basic pension and MIG levels will be to discourage further saving, especially among low-income workers.

To ameliorate the disincentive for workers whose retirement incomes are likely to be near or below the MIG to save, a pension credit was introduced in October 2003. Officially, the pension credit operates on the basis of a pound-for-pound withdrawal of means-tested benefit plus a 60 per cent savings credit, up to some maximum level of supplementary income. The maximum is currently set at £62 per week. Thus, as Clark and Emmerson (2003) point out, the calculation of pension credit can be regarded more simply as consisting of a 40 per cent rate of withdrawal on supplementary incomes up to the maximum. The capital rules which disqualified some people from receiving MIG payments do not apply, and the pension credit level will be uprated annually in line with earnings growth.

By reducing the means-tested penalty to 40 per cent for pensioners with modest amounts of supplementary income, the government hopes that the pension credit will raise substantially the level of retirement saving among workers with low to moderate earnings. If saving does rise, though, the

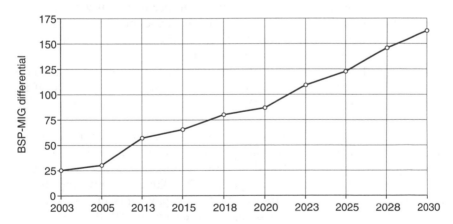

Figure 2.12.1 Increase in the MIG/BSP differential, £ per week, over time (author's calculations).

increase may not be as substantial as the government is hoping for. As Falkingham and Rake (2001) rightly point out, for the pension credit to raise savings, workers must understand how it rewards saving and adapt their behaviour accordingly. They must also believe that the reward for saving, which will not be realised until they retire, is worth the sacrifice of immediate consumption. Those who discount future consumption heavily – placing a much higher value on immediate consumption – may be unmoved by a reduction on the means-tested penalty from 100 to 40 per cent.

To determine the extent to which the pension credit makes saving worthwhile for them, workers need to be able to forecast accurately the proportion of their post-retirement incomes that will be subject to the 40 per cent rate of withdrawal. This will not be easy for two reasons. First, uncertainty about future returns to saving and annuity rates makes it diffi-cult to forecast accurately the level of supplementary income a person can expect to receive in retirement. Second, the gap between the basic pension and the level of income at which entitlement to pension credit is exhausted will widen over time, due to differences in indexation rates. If workers are unable to see with certainty that the pension credit will make them better off in retirement, they may conclude that the degree of uncertainty involved does not justify the reduction in current consumption associated with increased pension saving.

Access to suitable savings vehicles is essential if the pension credit is to give rise to increased discretionary retirement saving among low to moder-ate earners. Workers with incomes in the lower half of the income distrib-ution are especially likely to experience frequent changes of employer, part-time working and discontinuity of employment. As a result, they are less likely than other workers to have access to a good occupational pension scheme or to be served well by one. In so far as stakeholder pen-sions can be utilised along side, or in place of, occupational schemes, their introduction (discussed in Section 1.8) has made pension saving more accessible. Doubts remain, however, about the capacity of stakeholder pensions to deliver increased saving for retirement.

Cost and flexibility featured prominently in the design of stakeholder pensions. These plans would not be suitable for their target market if the relatively modest contributions that low- to middle-income earners could afford to make were eaten up by management charges. At the same time, a rigid contribution schedule would make them unsuitable for individuals with variable incomes. Accessibility would also be undermined if there were high set-up charges. The design that emerged was one featuring no set-up charges, with annual management fees limited to no more than 1 per cent of fund values. Although minimum payments into stakeholder pensions were set at £20, individuals are free to vary both the amount and timing of their contributions.

For stakeholder pensions to have a significant impact on the overall level of pension saving, take up needs to be high among low to moderate earners. In addition, these plans need to attract a substantial in-flow of funds. With no set-up charges, take up is likely to be higher than it would otherwise have been. Even so, concerns about liquidity and control are likely to limit the appeal of stakeholder pensions. The funds accumulated in these plans, like all pension savings, are not accessible before contributors reach pensionable age. Yet, liquidity considerations are likely to figure prominently in the savings decisions of workers with low to moderate earnings. Low to moderate earners may also regard the obligation to annuitise three-quarters of their accumulated funds as an unacceptable constraint on their freedom to use their savings as they see fit. Liquidity and control are likely to be of less concern for higher earners, since their opportunities to accumulate other forms of financial wealth alongside their pensions will be greater.

As Section 1.8 shows, over 750,000 stakeholder pensions were started in their first year of operation. Of these, though, 17 per cent, (128,000) were started on behalf of children, by individuals aged 65 and over, and by workers with above average earnings. Contributions to stakeholder plans averaged just £81 per month. Table 2.12.2 illustrates the sort of weekly retirement incomes that people making contributions of £81 per month might expect to generate. It is impossible to know how many of these plans, along with those which have been started subsequently, will continue to receive contributions until maturity. Faced with competing demands on their resources, many of those who have started a stakeholder pension, or will start one, may reduce the size and/or the frequency of their contributions. Others may lapse them altogether.

Confidence is a key determinant of people's willingness to undertake voluntary retirement saving through stakeholder plans or any other pensions vehicle. Yet in the 1990s confidence in private pensions was severely dented by events like the PPP mis-selling scandal, the Maxwell affair and the fiasco at Equitable Life. More recently, a rash of occupational scheme closures and wind-ups, reductions in annuity rates, and three years of falling equity values have cast further doubt upon the ability of private

Table 2.12.2 Weekly retirement income (£) generated by men and women making stakeholder contributions of £81 per month until age 65, by age at which contributions commence

	Men	*Women*
25	231	212
35	134	123
45	69	64
55	27	25

Source: Grainge *et al.* (2002).

pensions to deliver good retirement incomes. Against this background, new schemes and incentives may do little to boost discretionary retirement saving. Many people may be reluctant to increase their pension saving. Others may have decided to reduce the amounts they save, and some may have been scared off pension saving altogether.

In 1998, the government announced its intention to provide workers with personalised pension forecasts, (DSS 1998). These forecasts would give individuals accurate information about their current public and private pension positions. The official reason given for providing such information was that it would help people make better retirement saving decisions. Privately, though, the government must have been hoping that once people realised how small their pension incomes were likely to be, they would decide to increase their retirement saving. Producing these forecasts would be complex and expensive, and they have not so far materialised. Since April 2003, however, providers of money purchase plans have been required to issue their plan-holders with statutory money purchase illustrations (SMPIs).

SMPIs are projections showing how much retirement income at current prices an individual's existing pension savings would buy them at retirement. Although providers used to produce projections of future pension outcomes, these were not usually inflation-adjusted. SMPIs currently assume a 7 per cent annual rate of return to investments and 2.5 per cent inflation. They also assume that individuals take their pension at age 65. While SMPIs might motivate some workers to save more, they could have the opposite effect on others. If presented with low SMPI values, workers who are unable to save more may conclude that even their current level of pension saving is not worthwhile.

If the measures put in place by the present government to increase discretionary saving for retirement do not have their intended effect, a future government may look more favourably upon compulsion. An attraction of compulsion compared with voluntary saving is that its effects are immediate. It may also be more cost effective, in the short run at least. Raising pension saving on a voluntary basis can be costly, because the required incentives may involve substantial tax expenditures. In addition, where incentives are complex, workers may require expensive public information programmes in order to understand them. Even if incentives succeed in raising voluntary saving, it may take a long time before their effects are fully realised. Compulsion would not be problem-free, however.

Forcing, rather than persuading, people to undertake supplementary pension saving may arouse political resentment. Compulsory pension contributions are likely to be viewed by the electorate as just another tax. To win political acceptance, the government might need to provide pension benefit guarantees which, in the long run, could prove very expensive. Compulsion might be particularly problematic for young workers for whom pensions constitute only one of a number of saving objectives.

Other saving objectives of young workers include education and house purchase. What is more, compulsion could have perverse effects. As Segars (2002) notes, it may simply lead people to reduce the amounts they save voluntarily. In this case, the effect of compulsion on overall pension saving might be neutral, or even negative.

2.13 SIMPLIFYING PENSIONS

When, in the early 1980s, British governments began to worry about how to meet the perceived threat to Britain's PAYG public pension arrangements arising from population ageing, the answer seemed clear enough. An expansion of private pension provision could compensate for the cuts in public pension payments that would be necessary if state spending on retired people was to be kept to an acceptable proportion of GDP. Most of this expansion would have to take the form of extra individual saving for retirement. Although half the workforce was not covered by an occupational pension, occupational scheme coverage was not expected to increase (DHSS 1985). Nearly two decades later, concerns about the adequacy and security of private provision led the government to launch three separate but related pension reviews. The Inland Revenue was instructed to carry out a review of the tax treatment of private pensions. In addition, Alan Pickering and Ron Sandler were appointed to head their own reviews of occupational pensions and medium to long-term saving, including individual retirement saving.

The aim of all three reviews was the same; to identify ways in which the particular aspect of Britain's pension arrangements under review might be simplified. The reasons for setting up the reviews are set out in the Green Paper (DWP 2002). Essentially, Britain's pension arrangements had become excessively complex. There were eight different tax regimes for pensions. This imposed an unnecessary administrative burden on pension providers and constrained individual choice by making pensions difficult to understand and explain. The need to comply with a mass of other regulation was making it increasingly difficult for employers to provide their workers with good occupational pensions. In addition, individual saving was being undermined by complex products which were difficult to compare and where the costs of advice were often prohibitive for product providers and their customers.

Of the three reviews, Ron Sandler's review of medium and long-term saving was the first to report, on 9 July 2002. Pickering reported two days later. The report of the Inland Revenue's review of pensions taxation (Inland Revenue 2002) did not appear until November. In his report (Sandler 2002) Sandler, a former chief executive of Lloyd's of London, suggested that due to weak competition, medium to long-term savings products were often expensive and offered poor value for money.

Moreover, the complexity of products and the high costs of advice constituted an especially strong impediment to long-term saving – including retirement saving – amongst low- to middle-income groups. Sandler recommended that a range of simplified savings products be introduced, which could be bought without the need for expensive advice. These products would be modelled on the new stakeholder pensions, having no up-front commissions, with charges limited to 1 per cent of savers' funds.

Although some in the financial services industry questioned the ability of commercial companies to make a profit in the '1 per cent world' proposed by Sandler, the Sandler Report was generally well received. Proposals for simplifying the taxation of private pensions contained in the report of the Inland Revenue review provoked more controversy. In particular, doubts have been expressed about the desirability of replacing annual limits on the tax relief applied to pension contributions and investment returns with a lifetime exemption for funds up to a maximum value of £1.4 million. Treasury plans to impose a 60 per cent tax penalty on funds with values in excess of £1.4 million have also been criticised. Of the three reports, though, the report of the Pickering Review (Pickering 2002) was probably the least well received.

Pickering, a former Chairman of the NAPF, produced a report containing more than 50 recommendations. The picture of Britain's occupational pension arrangements that it presented was one of too many different types of scheme wieghed down by a mass of costly and often unnecessary regulation. While some employers were responding to the mounting burden of regulation by closing their pension schemes, others were being put off starting them. At the same time, workers' pension choices were obscured by differences in the rules applying to the various scheme types and by regulatory restrictions relating to concurrency – the simultaneous participation in two or more different schemes. Pickering's recommendations were mainly aimed at streamlining occupational pension provision. He proposed that the number of different types of scheme should be reduced – from more than 20 to just two or three – and that some aspects of regulation should be eased so as to reduce the costs of compliance.

Some of Pickering's recommendations were widely applauded. Among these were his proposals for the abolition of vesting periods, and for OPRA to be replaced with a more proactive pensions regulator. His report was attacked, however, for the way in which it proposed to reduce employers' costs of providing salary-related pensions and for the narrowness of its focus. To cut the cost of providing DB pensions, Pickering proposed that schemes should no longer have to provide limited price indexation of pension benefits, and nor should they have to pay pensions to the spouses of deceased workers. He also proposed that benefit formulas might be reduced, so that pension entitlements would, in the future, accrue more slowly.

The trades unions were outraged by Pickering's proposals. They regarded the suggestion that schemes should be made cheaper for employers by reducing the benefits they offered as an attack on working people and a recipe for pensioner poverty. The government was not much more enthusiastic. Quoted in the *Financial Times*, Andrew Smith – then Work and Pensions Secretary – described Pickering's proposals on spouse's benefits and inflation-proofing as going against a 30-year drive to enhance survivors' benefits and price protect pensions (*Financial Times* 2002). Seventeen months later, though, the government announced in the Queen's Speech that it would legislate to reduce the level of benefit indexation from its current maximum of 5 per cent to just 2.5 per cent.

Pickering was accused of adopting too narrow a focus because costly regulations were only one aspect of complexity in Britain's pension arrangements. Complexity also existed due to the complicated ways in which private pensions interacted with the different forms of state pension provision. Too often, public and private provision overlapped in ways that raised providers' administrative costs and created confusion for workers. The complexity arising from the increased use of means-testing of state retirement benefits needed to be tackled urgently. Pickering's critics argued that, by focusing on just one piece of the pensions jigsaw, he had missed a golden opportunity to make proposals for much more radical reform of Britain's pension system.

An example of a simple pension system – one that many advocates of fundamental reform believe that Britain would do well to emulate – is provided by Australia. Since 1992, the Australian pension system has combined a flat-rate means-tested state pension with compulsory occupational pension provision. Although means-testing has been a feature of the country's pension arrangements since public pensions were introduced in 1909, until 1992 the provision of occupational pensions had been voluntary. In the 1980s, the pattern of occupational scheme membership was very similar to that in the UK. Around 50 per cent of Australian workers were members of occupational schemes (Banks *et al.* 2002). Participation was much lower among women than it was among men. Overall, coverage was greatest amongst public sector workers and low amongst employees of small firms. Today, virtually all Australian employees are covered by an occupational scheme.

The move to compulsory occupational pension provision was the result of an agreement between the Australian government, employers and the trades unions that employers should make mandatory pension contributions on behalf of their employees. A series of legislative changes, culminating in the 1992 Superannuation Guarantee Charge (SGC), has made participation in an employer-provided DC pension scheme both a right and a condition of employment for all but the lowest-paid Australian employees. Initially, employers' contributions, which were scheduled to rise over time, were set at 3 per cent of earnings. In 1997–1998, the contribution rate stood at 6 per cent (King *et al.* 2001). By 2002–2003, it had reached its target level of 9 per cent. Although a proposal to compel employees to contribute 3 per cent of their earnings to their superannuation plans was dropped in the late 1990s, fiscal incentives ensure that around half of all workers make contributions on a voluntary basis.

An interesting feature of Australia's 1992 reform was the ease with which the switch from voluntary to compulsory occupational pensions was made. The SGC legislation was widely supported by workers and their employers. The reason seems to have been that each of the parties to the agreement believed that they stood to gain from it. Australia's powerful labour unions had been campaigning for some time for higher pay and an extension of occupational scheme coverage. Employers were prepared to go along with mandatory pension contributions because, as a *quid pro quo*, the unions agreed to moderate their current and future pay claims. From the government's perspective, the agreement offered the prospect of a reduction, over time, in the amounts being paid out in state pension payments.

As Davis (1995) notes, the low level of state pension provision in Australia also helped to ensure trade union support for the 1992 reform. Australia's state pension scheme, which was unaltered by the SGC legislation, is a basic income scheme paying flat-rate retirement benefits financed out of general taxation. Pensions are currently payable to men aged 65 and women aged 61, and are subject to a 10-year residency requirement and a means test. As in Britain, however, male and female retirement ages are currently being equalised in stages, and will be 65 for both sexes in 2013. For Australians with full benefit entitlement, the state provides a level of income replacement equal to around 25 per cent of average male earnings. Although this is more generous than income replacement from Britain's BSP, the effective rate of replacement can be very low for retiring workers with earned incomes above the national average.

Making Britain's pension arrangements resemble those in Australia would require legislation which would sweep away the existing array of public and private supplementary schemes and replace it with a uniform set of mandatory occupational DC plans. This would create a one-off cost to the exchequer, since a sum equal to the actuarial value of workers' accrued entitlements from SERPS and S2P would have to be transferred into their DC plans. Similarly, the actuarial value of workers' accrued rights in occupational DB schemes would have to be paid into their DC plans. This could be very costly for firms with under-funded DB schemes. Although these transitional costs for firms and the exchequer would not be trivial, they may be worth paying when set against the potential benefits of such a reform.

An obvious benefit of such a reform would be consistency of treatment. As well as accruing rights to a pension from the BSP, all workers would be accumulating retirement savings in an employer's DC plan. Moreover, the simplicity of the system might be expected to have a positive impact on individuals' willingness to undertake additional voluntary retirement saving. In addition, efficiency improvements would arise due to enhanced labour market flexibility. As long as transfers of funds between employers' plans were free – or subject to a relatively low administrative charge which was unrelated to fund values, the new system would be free from the disincentives to labour mobility inherent in the existing arrangements.

Legislation to replace Britain's existing supplementary pension arrangements with mandatory employer-provided DC plans could also improve the financing position of the BSP. Instead of reducing NI contributions to compensate for the scrapping of the state supplementary schemes, the portion of workers' NICs that would have gone to SERPS/S2P – or to contracted-out occupational and personal pensions – could be used to fund the BSP. This might be made politically acceptable if the value of BSP payments was raised to the cut-off level for pension credit. This would remove means testing from Britain's pension arrangements, and the resulting administrative savings would help to defray the higher cost of the BSP. BSP revenues would be further strengthened if, in order to reverse the trend towards early retirement, the qualifying age for mandatory employers' DC pensions was set equal to the SPA.

An interesting, though much more radical, idea for the reform and simplification of British pensions was put forward by Falkingham and Johnson more than a decade ago (Falkingham and Johnson 1993). Their idea was for a single or unified system of earnings-related funded pensions with a minimum level of tax-financed pension provision. Such a scheme – one they called a unified funded pension scheme (UFPS) – would, they argued, 'facilitate saving for old age and prevent pensioner poverty'. It would involve all workers making compulsory contributions equal to a fixed proportion of their pre-tax earnings to DC personal retirement funds (PRFs). These PRFs would be managed by a number of competing providers, and transfers between providers would be free. The amounts contributed would be the actuarial amounts necessary to produce a fund capable of providing a pension equal to some fraction of average earnings (e.g. 50 per cent) at retirement age.

To ensure that low earners and those with no earnings were able to accumulate adequate pensions, these individuals would have an annual capital transfer to their PRF financed out of general taxation sufficient to maintain its required growth trajectory. Thus, the UFPS would unite earnings-related funded pensions and PAYG pension provision in a single scheme. Unlike conventional PAYG arrangements, however, the PAYG element of the UFPS would involve intrapersonal rather than intergenerational redistribution of income. Another feature of a UFPS might be an element of smoothing to PRF investment returns – or some other form of asset market insurance – to protect those approaching retirement age from adverse movements in the value of their PRF investments.

An important distinction between the approaches to simplification outlined above – an Australian style reform and the introduction of a UFPS –

concerns the state's commitment to pension provision. In the former case, PAYG pensions would continue to be paid directly through the state. In the case of a UFPS, the state's commitment to pension provision would be indirect. With a UFPS, the state would, in effect, underwrite workers' private pension savings rather than provide them with pension payments when they retired. The common feature in both approaches is that they combine compulsory DC pension saving with an element of state provision. As Section 2.3 notes, DC funded schemes are capital-market based and PAYG schemes are labour-market based. Combining elements of both in an Australian-style or UFPS reform would allow workers to take advantage of the low (but relatively certain) returns available from a PAYG scheme and the less certain – but potentially greater – returns available to funding.

A feature of both approaches to simplification is the presence of transition costs. With an Australian-style reform, the government would have to buy out workers' accrued pension rights from SERPS/S2P by transferring a sum equivalent to the actuarial value of these entitlements into individuals' PRFs. The introduction of a UFPS would involve the government in the much greater cost of buying out workers' accrued BSP entitlements as well. Because a government's PAYG obligations must always be honoured, or bought-out, transition costs cannot be avoided during a switch, whether in part or in full, from PAYG to funded pensions. These costs may be worth paying, however, if sticking with the current level of PAYG provision would give rise to even greater costs due to adverse demographic conditions.

Part 3

An A–Z of Pensions

Aaron–Samuelson condition: derives its name from developments in the theory of pensions advanced by Henry Aaron and Paul Samuelson. It states that individuals will be better off contributing to an unfunded pension scheme, rather than saving for retirement through a funded scheme, if the implicit return to contributions to the unfunded scheme is greater than the rate of return on financial assets. The implicit return to contributions to an unfunded scheme equals the rate of growth of total earnings; the growth rate of earnings plus the rate of growth of the labour force. An unfunded scheme is likely to be superior, then, at times of rapid population growth, since the implicit return on contributions will be high. When population growth is low, the rate of return on the financial assets held in a funded scheme is likely to exceed the growth rate of total earnings. In this case, individuals would do better to save for retirement through a funded scheme. A criticism of the Aaron–Samuelson condition is that it takes no account of increases in life expectancy, which tend to reduce the rate of return to funded schemes and increase the implicit return to contributions to unfunded schemes. It also takes no account of the relative risks of funded and unfunded schemes. See also **Money's Worth Ratio**.

Accelerated accrual: the ability to accrue pension rights in a DB scheme more rapidly than the scheme's normal accrual rate.

Accrual rate: the rate at which pension rights build up for each year of pensionable service in a DB scheme. Typical accrual rates for UK DB occupational schemes are a sixtieth and an eightieth of final salary. Thus a worker with 20 years pensionable service would have accrued pension rights worth either a third or a quarter of their final salary, depending on their scheme's accrual rate.

Accrued pension: the value of pension rights – vested or otherwise – accrued in a DB scheme up to a given point prior to retirement. A worker's accrued pension can be calculated on the basis of his or her current earnings, as though the worker had left the scheme, or in relation to projected future earnings.

Accumulated Benefit Obligation (ABO): the value of a DB scheme's liabilities if it were to be wound up immediately. A scheme's liabilities consist of pensions in payment, the preserved pensions of former members and the accrued benefit rights of current contributors. See also **Projected benefit obligation**.

Accumulation phase: the period prior to annuitisation in DC schemes, during which individuals accumulate a fund from a combination of contributions and investment returns.

Actively managed fund: a fund comprised of assets which are traded regularly in order to make capital gains from short-term changes in market prices. The investment returns earned depend upon the skill, and/or luck, of the fund managers. Pension schemes with actively managed funds have high administration charges due to the high dealing costs they incur. See also **Index tracker fund; Passive fund**.

Active members: the contributors to a pension scheme who are accruing entitlements to future retirement benefits. In the case of occupational schemes, active members will also be employees of the sponsoring firm.

Actuarial assumptions: the assumptions on which actuarial valuations of DB schemes are based. These include assumptions about the numbers of workers joining and leaving a scheme; rates of return on the scheme's financial assets, such as equities, government bonds and property; earnings growth; life expectancy of scheme members, etc. Changes to any of the assumptions used can have a significant effect on the outcome of an actuarial valuation.

Actuarial fairness: the principle whereby the expected present value of pension benefits should be equal to the present value of contributions. It is because of this principle that individuals with diminished life expectancies are able to obtain higher than average annuity rates.

Actuarial valuation: an assessment, by an actuary, of whether the assets in a DB pension scheme are adequate to meet its current and future liabilities.

Actuary: a specialist in estimating and valuing mortality risk. Actuaries determine, among other things, life assurance policy premiums, the appropriate level of contributions to DB pension schemes and the rates payable on different types of annuity contract. See also **Gompertz**.

Added years (service credits): extra years of notional membership of a DB scheme added to individuals' actual years of pensionable service, thereby increasing the retirement benefits they are entitled to receive. Schemes often permit members to purchase additional years of scheme membership at full actuarial cost to the purchaser. Extra years of pensionable service can also be bought from AVCs or a transfer payment from another scheme, or be added through augmentation. See also **Additional Voluntary Contributions; Enhancements; Transfer value**.

Additional Voluntary Contributions (AVCs): contributions to a DB occupational pension scheme that members can elect to pay in addition to their normal contributions. AVCs accumulate in a separately managed fund, the terminal value of which is used to purchase additional retirement, disability or death benefits from the occupational scheme. Under current rules, the total value of contributions – normal plus AVCs – must not exceed 15 per cent of earnings. Although all members are free to make AVCs, they are one way that late starters, and those with contributions gaps, can boost their pension rights. See also **Free-Standing Additional Voluntary Contributions**.

Administration charges: charges levied by pension providers to cover their administration costs. These can include one-off set-up and exit fees and ongoing management charges, where the amounts charged may be flat rate, or proportional to contributions, investment returns or annual fund values. See also **Charge ratio; Reduction in yield**.

Administration costs: the costs incurred in administering a pension scheme. These arise from the need to employ labour and capital in the collection of contributions, maintenance of records and payment of benefits. Funded schemes will incur fund management costs and, where there is competition amongst providers, advertising and marketing costs will also be incurred. Public schemes benefit from economies of scale and, because membership is usually compulsory, they do not incur advertising and marketing costs. Consequently, they typically have lower administration costs than private schemes.

Advance Corporation Tax (ACT): a tax paid by UK companies on the dividends they distribute to shareholders. See also **Dividend Tax Credits**.

Adverse selection: a situation where insurance contracts are only purchased by those who are most likely to benefit from them. The price of insurance contracts will be higher in markets where adverse selection is present, because it reduces insurers' ability to earn profits by pooling risk.

Age-specific life expectancy: the average number of additional years a person of a particular age can expect to live.

Age-specific mortality rate: the number of deaths – usually in a year – among people of a particular age, expressed as a proportion of all individuals of that age.

Age-related benefits: benefits which people become entitled to receive solely because of their age. Since the poorest pensioners in Britain tend to be the oldest, the provision of age-related benefits, such as free TV licences, is seen as a means of targeting help on those who need it most.

Annua: annuity contracts available in Roman times. These contracts allowed individuals to receive a stream of income payments for a fixed term in return for a single upfront payment.

Annuitisation: the transformation of a capital sum into a stream of income through the purchase of an annuity. Annuitisation can be voluntary or, as in the case of funds accrued in UK individual pension plans, mandatory. See also **Compulsory annuitization, Open market option**.

Annuity: a contract whereby a provider, normally an insurance company, agrees to provide an individual with a stream of income, usually until death, in return for an initial capital sum. Annuities are thus a form of private sector longevity insurance. Annuities can be purchased on either a single or joint life basis. They are of three general types – level annuities, paying a fixed nominal income; escalating annuities, where the income is periodically increased according to a fixed formula; and indexed annuities, where the amount of income received increases in line with annual changes in a cost of living index such as the UK's retail price index. See also **Annuitisation, Annuity rate**.

Annuity factor: a measure of the value of an annuity calculated as the sum of the discounted values of expected payments minus the original purchase price.

Annuity rate: the nominal value of annuity payments expressed as a percentage of an annuity's lump-sum cost. Rates are often quoted as £X per year for every £10,000 invested. Thus, the rate on an annuity paying £620 per annum for every £10,000 invested would be 6.2 per cent. Except where the law requires them to be equal, annuity rates for females are lower than those for males, reflecting women's greater longevity. Conversely, rate enhancements are usually available to smokers and other groups with diminished life expectancies, such as the terminally ill, through so-called impaired life annuities. Because annuities are usually backed by government bonds, rates vary over time, reflecting changes in the rates of return on these financial instruments. Changes in the average life expectancy of the population, or a subgroup of it, also cause annuity rates to vary. See also **Annuity**.

Approved Personal Pension (APP): a personal pension plan which has approval under the UK's contracting-out rules to receive a rebate of part of the planholder's NICs. See also **Rebate only personal pension**.

Asset allocation: the proportions of a pension fund held in different classes of asset – equities, bonds, property, cash, etc. The choice of which assets to hold, and the quantities in which they are held, will depend upon factors such as the schemes needed for capital growth or income, the fund manager's judgement about the future prospects for particular asset types, regulation and taxation. See also **Asset-liability matching; Dividend Tax Credits; Financial Reporting Standard 17**.

Asset-liability matching: an approach to ass*et al*location whereby assets with different revenue-generating characteristics are selected so as to match the liability structure of a DB funded pension scheme. Typically, assets with high growth potential will be matched with a scheme's distant, and therefore uncertain, liabilities. More immediate liabilities must be matched with assets which yield a stable and predictable revenue stream. Cash and fixed interest or index-linked bonds match a scheme's most immediate liability, its current pensions bill. Equities match long-term liabilities, the pension rights currently being accrued by active members.

Deferred annuities can be matched with the future liabilities represented by preserved pensions.

Asset reversion: the payment of part or all of the surplus funds in a funded DB occupational scheme to the sponsoring employer. See also **Over-funded scheme**.

Augmentation: extra years of pensionable service sometimes awarded to members of DB occupational schemes, the cost of which is borne by the scheme and/or the sponsoring employer. See also **Added years**.

Average final salary scheme: a DB scheme where pension benefits are calculated as a fixed fraction of a person's average earnings in the years just before retirement, multiplied by years of service. Thus, benefits might be calculated as one-sixtieth of average salary in the three years leading up to retirement, for each year of service.

Back-loading: the term denoting the way in which the value of benefits in final salary schemes accrues more rapidly as employees approach retirement age. This is because salary increases received later in an individual's working life are combined with more years of pensionable service compared with pay increases received earlier on. An effect of back-loading is, therefore, to penalise early leavers and reward long-stayers. Back-loading can thus have a powerful disincentive effect on employees' willingness to change jobs – especially older workers – and can thereby undermine the efficient operation of the labour market.

Basic State Pension (BSP): the flat-rate virtually universal public pension in the UK. By itself, the BSP does not provide an adequate level of retirement income. In April 2003, the BSP was set at £77.45 per week for a single pensioner and £123.80 for a couple, well below the official old age poverty line of £102.10 and £155.80 respectively.

Beneficiaries: see **Members**.

Beveridge (Lord William Henry, 1879–1963): an economist, journalist, civil servant and, for a short time, Liberal Member of Parliament for the constituency of Berwick-on-Tweed. Educated at Charterhouse and Balliol College Oxford, he was Director of the London School of Economics from 1919 to 1937. As Chairman of the Social Service Inquiry of 1941–1942 he produced the famous 'Beveridge Report', properly entitled Social Insurance and Allied Services. The report, on which the welfare state reforms of the mid- to late-1940s were based, proposed a safety-net system of cradle to grave social insurance. Beveridge believed that poverty was mainly the result of unemployment, sickness and old age. Consequently, his proposals were for a contributory social insurance system that would insure individuals against poverty arising from these contingencies throughout their entire lives.

Bismarck (Prince Otto Von, 1815–1898): known as the Iron Chancellor, Bismark was largely responsible for the unification of Germany in 1871. He also established the world's first public pension scheme in 1889. It was a contributory social insurance scheme with a retirement age of 70, which provided earnings-linked pension benefits in return for earnings-related contributions. Bismarck was dismissed by Wilhelm II in 1890.

Blackley (Canon William Lewery, 1830–1902): a clergyman and pioneer of public pensions in Britain, who, for more than a decade, campaigned for the introduction of a system of national provident insurance to cover workers against poverty arising from sickness and old age. Blackley's proposals, which were never implemented, required workers between the ages of 18 and 21 to contribute to a common fund which would be used to provide sickness benefits and retirement pensions.

Book reserve scheme: an unfunded occupational pension scheme where workers' pension rights are a direct liability of the sponsoring firm and where retirement benefits are paid for from the sponsor's operating revenues. The pension rights of workers in book reserve schemes are often indemnified with an insurance company to cover against the failure of the sponsoring firm. Although these schemes are common in Germany and Japan, in many countries they are outlawed.

Career Average Revalued Earnings (CARE) scheme: a career average scheme where, in order to calculate retirement benefits, earnings in a worker's penultimate year of service and all preceding years are inflation adjusted. Thus, other things being equal, pensions from CARE schemes will be larger than those from a simple career average scheme, but smaller than those from a final salary scheme. A return to career averaged pensions is seen by some as a way to rescue DB occupational schemes from their current financing difficulties. See **Career average scheme**.

Career average scheme: a DB occupational pension scheme where retirement benefits are calculated as a fixed fraction of an employee's earnings averaged up to retirement multiplied by their years of service. Career average schemes can be provided more cheaply than final salary schemes, because the retirement benefits workers receive are lower. Nevertheless, in the 1970s many British companies replaced their career average schemes with final salary schemes.

Charge ratio (reduction in premium): a measure of the reduction in terminal fund values of DC schemes resulting from administrative charges. The charge ratio compares the value of individuals' funds at retirement with the amount they could have accumulated if administrative charges could be avoided. Thus, the terminal funds of schemes with a 30 per cent charge ratio will be 30 per cent lower than they would have been if there were no administrative charges.

Cliff-vesting: a common feature of DB occupational schemes whereby an employee must have been a scheme member for a period of time before becoming eligible to receive retirement benefits. Cliff-vesting is much less common in DC schemes. In the United States, for example, cliff-vesting is a feature of virtually all DB schemes, whereas around 70 per cent of DC schemes have immediate vesting. See also **Vesting period**.

Cohort: a group of individuals who were born in the same year.

Commutation: the conversion of part or all of a person's future annuity payments into an immediate lump sum. See also **Guaranteed annuities**.

Company pension scheme: see **Occupational scheme**.

Comprehensive income tax: a tax regime which taxes all income sources equally. No distinction is made between income for consumption and income for saving. Because income from investment returns is taxed as well as earnings, a comprehensive income tax drives the post-tax return to savings below the pre-tax return. There is thus a disincentive to save, since immediate consumption is worth more than consumption in the future. A comprehensive income tax is, therefore, regarded as an inappropriate regime for the taxation of pension savings.

Compulsory annuitisation: the legal requirement, in some countries, for members of DC schemes to use all, or part, of their terminal fund to purchase an annuity. The justification for compulsion is usually that because individuals have received tax relief on their pension contributions, the government has a legitimate say in how their terminal fund is used. Under current rules, contributors to individual pension plans must annuitise at least 75 per cent of their terminal fund between the ages of 55 and 70. Although compulsory annuitisation ensures that contributors to individual pensions have a stream of income for the rest of their lives, the practice is controversial. Individuals are denied the possibility of obtaining higher returns from alternative investments. What's more, because annuitisation, unlike other forms of investment, involves the exchange of capital for income, compulsion is likely to be particularly problematic for lower-income groups. The members of higher-income groups are more likely to have additional forms of wealth from which to make discretionary investments and/or bequests. See also **Annuitisation, Open market option, Voluntary annuities**.

Concurrency (concomitance): the ability to contribute to two or more pension schemes at the same time. Concurrency makes it possible for workers to optimise their pension saving by contributing to a variety of schemes that have offsetting risks and returns. It also makes it possible for contributors to schemes which have contribution limits to undertake additional pension saving.

Contracted-out rebate: the reduction in the rate of NICs made by members of a contracted-out DB pension scheme and their employers and the proportion of NICS made by contributors to contracted-out DC schemes and their employers which is rebated to their schemes.

Contracted-out scheme: a UK pension scheme the members of which opt out of SERPS or the second state pension. In return for giving up their right to a pension from SERPS or S2P, members of DB schemes and their employers make NICs at a reduced rate. Contributors to contracted-out DC schemes, along with their employers, make full NICs, a portion of which is then rebated to their schemes.

Contractual retirement age: the age at which an employee must retire, which is specified in their contract of employment. Contractual retirement ages can be justified in occupations where the decline in peoples' faculties due to ageing would make employment beyond a certain age unsafe. In 2002, the British government announced its intention to outlaw compulsory retirement on grounds of age, where it is practical to do so.

Contribution rate: the amount of money workers and/or their employers contribute to a pension scheme, expressed as a proportion of pensionable earnings. Where workers and their employers contribute, contribution rates are not necessarily the same for both parties. See also **Employer's contributions**.

Contributions: payments by a worker and/or his or her employer into a contributory pension scheme. Contributions, which are normally exempt from income tax, can be either flat rate, with all contributors paying the same, or earnings related, such that those who earn more contribute more. See also **Contribution rate**.

Contributions holiday: a period during which workers and/or their employers make no pension contributions. Contributions holidays are often taken where a funded DB scheme is in actuarial surplus.

Contributory pension scheme: a scheme into which workers must make financial contributions during their working lives in order to obtain a pension at retirement. Some schemes require only workers or their employers to make contributions. Many schemes, however, require both workers and their employers to contribute. See also **Employee's contributions; Employer's contributions**.

Coverage: the number of workers who are members of a pension scheme, expressed as a proportion of all workers. Even where membership of a scheme is compulsory, as with many public schemes, coverage can be less than 100 per cent if participation is not obligatory for all individuals of working age and/or workers are free to join an alternative scheme. Where membership is voluntary, coverage will reflect the extent to which schemes are made available to workers and the level of take-up. For example, in the UK occupational scheme coverage is less than 50 per cent because not all employers offer a pension scheme and not all workers join one where it is offered.

Covered earnings: earnings on which pension contributions are payable and/or on which DB pension benefits are based. Covered earnings may include all income from employment, or may be restricted to a portion of total earnings. See also **Lower earnings limit; Upper earnings limit**.

Crude death rate: a measure of the number of deaths occurring annually in a population. See: **Death rate; Infant mortality rate.**

Death benefits (survivors benefits): benefits received by the financial dependents of pensioners who have died, usually a half or some other fraction of the deceased pensioner's pension.

Death-in-service benefits: lump sum benefits payable to the spouses or dependents of currently active members of a pension scheme upon their death.

Death rate: the number of deaths per thousand people in a population within a given time period, usually one year. 'Crude death rates' relate to the number of deaths in an entire population. In Japan, for example, 1,012,400 people died in the year 2000, out of a total population of 126,550,000. Thus the crude death rate was 1,012,400 divided by 126,550,000 times 1,000, which equals 8. In the same year, the crude death rates for Canada, America and the UK were respectively 7, 9 and 10. Death rates are frequently calculated for population subgroups. Age-specific death rates, for example, are measures of the number of deaths per thousand people in a population of a given age. These are often calculated separately for males and females. Death rates at all ages differ between social classes, types of occupation, smokers and non-smokers, and married and single people. See also **Infant mortality rate.**

Deferred annuitisation: the decision of a member of a DC scheme to postpone the annuitisation of their terminal fund. In the UK, contributors to DC plans have until age 75 to annuitise their accumulated funds. Deferring annuitisation can make sense for individuals with above-average life expectancies, since annuity rates increase with the age of the annuitant. See also **Income drawdown**.

Deferred annuity: an annuity contract where the benefits to be paid do not begin until a date subsequent to the date of purchase. In the UK, deferred annuities are used to secure active members' accrued pension rights when DB schemes are wound up.

Deferred pensioners: former employees of a firm who have entitlements to future pension benefits from its occupational scheme in respect of their periods of employment. See also **Preserved pension rights**.

Deficiency payment: a payment into a funded DB scheme by the sponsoring employer to reduce or eliminate an actuarial deficit. Deficiency payments may take the form of a single one-off payment or a stream of smaller payments made over time. For example, it was reported in May 2003 that Castings, a UK manufacturer of truck, car and rail components, had decided to make a £4 million payment into its pension scheme in order to eliminate a deficit of that amount.

Deficit correction period: the length of time an under-funded scheme is given to return to 100 per cent funding. For example, the 1995 Pensions Act required moderately under-funded schemes to return to full funding within three years. If the deficit correction period is too long it will fail to provide adequate protection for scheme members. On the other hand, too short a period could also harm scheme members if cash-starved firms only have a short time in which to make large payments to their pension schemes. See also **Minimum funding requirement**.

Defined Benefit (DB) scheme: a pension scheme which guarantees to provide members with a specific amount of retirement income defined by a benefit formula. Benefits may be flat rate or earnings-related, and DB schemes may be funded or financed on a PAYG basis. Flat-rate schemes pay a fixed amount of pension benefit for each year of membership. Earnings-related schemes pay benefits the value of which are determined with reference to a member's final or average salary and years of membership. Thus, a DB scheme may provide a retiring worker with a pension equal to one-sixtieth or one-eightieth of his or her salary at retirement for each year of membership.

Defined Contribution (DC) scheme (money purchase scheme): a pension scheme which specifies the amounts that members must contribute to a pension fund. The value of the retirement benefits members ultimately receive depends upon the amounts contributed, the period over which contributions are made, the investment returns earned and available annuity rates. DC schemes may be provided on an individual or a group basis. Because they do not contain a specific benefits promise, DC schemes can be a cheaper way than DB schemes for employers to provide their workers with occupational pensions.

Delayed Retirement Credit (DRC): an increase in pension benefits available to American workers who work beyond the normal retirement age. The DRC was originally set at 3 per cent for each year of pension deferral, but is gradually being increased. It will eventually reach 8 per cent for those born after 1943. Similar benefit enhancements are available to workers in Britain.

De minimis pension: an amount of pension income that is so small that it may, under UK rules, be commuted to a cash sum. In 2002, pensions of up to £260 per annum were de minimis.

Demographic transition: a shift, over time, in the age structure of a population. Most developed countries have experienced a demographic transition from a situation where the young dominate to one where the largest group in the population consists of older people.

Directly invested scheme: see **Self-administered scheme**.

Disability benefits: pension benefits payable to individuals who are forced to retire before their scheme's normal retirement age due to disability.

Disclosure: the provision of relevant information to those with an interest in a pension scheme (its members, trustees, etc.) or anyone who may come to have an interest in it. Following the Maxwell affair, the disclosure rules for UK occupational schemes were tightened in the hope that increased transparency would help to prevent a similar scandal. Robert Maxwell was able to rob his companies' pensioners by keeping them and their trustees ignorant of their scheme's true financial position. Subsequent to the PPP mis-selling fiasco, the disclosure rules relating to individual pensions were also strengthened. Clarity is a key aspect of disclosure. Thus, there is now a requirement for providers of PPP and stakeholder plans to give potential customers full information on the costs and likely benefits of their products in language that is clear and straightforward.

Discontinuance valuation: a way of valuing funded DB schemes which compares the value of assets a scheme would need to hold in order to cover all its liabilities if it were to be wound up, with the actual assets held. The solvency position of a scheme which is valued using this approach depends upon the timing of the valuation, because discontinuance valuations are based on the current market prices of a scheme's assets. Other things being equal, a valuation made when asset prices are depressed will show a larger deficit or smaller surplus than would have been revealed under more buoyant asset market conditions. The discontinuance approach is probably the right way to value mature schemes where the sponsor is vulnerable to bankruptcy. For younger schemes with financially secure sponsors, the ongoing approach to valuation may be more appropriate, because it takes account of asset market volatility and allows for increases in asset values over time.

Discounted transfer value: the reduced cash equivalent of an individual's accrued pension rights in an under-funded DB scheme. If a scheme is only 70 per cent funded, members transferring to another scheme will only take with them 70 per cent of the full value of their accrued pension rights. See also **Transfer value**.

Discretionary increase: an increase in the value of a pension in payment or a preserved pension to which the recipient is not automatically entitled under the rules of their scheme. Discretionary increases are sometimes granted in order to reduce actuarial surpluses in DB occupational pension schemes.

Dividend Tax Credits (DTCs): an arrangement in existence until mid-1997, whereby UK funded pension schemes could reclaim the advance corporation tax paid on the dividend income they receive from equity investments. This tax perk was worth around £5 billion a year. By reducing the return on schemes' equity investments, abolition of dividend tax credits has raised the funding rate required to achieve a given fund size. Consequently, employers now find it more expensive to provide their workers with DB occupational schemes, and contributors to money purchase plans must now contribute more, or accept lower terminal funds.

Double dipping: disposing of tax-privileged pension savings in order to qualify for means-tested welfare benefits paid for by taxpayers. The potential for double dipping is greatest where annuitisation is entirely voluntary, or where part of a person's pension savings may be taken as a lump sum.

Early leavers: individuals who leave an occupational pension scheme before the official retirement age. They may do this due to a change of employer, redundancy or enforced retirement resulting from illness or disability. Early leavers from DB plans can suffer a number of problems which are not experienced by long stayers. Those who leave during their scheme's vesting period will lose all their accrued pension entitlements. Others may incur sizeable charges when transferring their entitlements to another employer's scheme or to a personal pension plan. Where transfers into another scheme are not made, early leavers cannot access their pension entitlements before reaching the scheme's official retirement age. Where entitlements are preserved, early leavers can end up effectively subsidising other workers who stay to retirement, through the investment returns on their contributions. Women are especially susceptible to early-leaver problems because they tend to change jobs more frequently and have shorter average job tenure than men.

Early retirement: premature withdrawal from employment, i.e. before a scheme's official or normal retirement age. Many schemes permit members to retire early, with no loss of benefits, on grounds of ill health. It is not uncommon for employers to offer older workers early retirement as an alternative to redundancy. Early retirement is thought to be a major factor in declining labour market participation amongst older workers, especially men. See also **Normal retirement age**.

Earnings cap: an upper limit on income from which tax-free pension contributions may be made. In the fiscal year 2002–2003, employee contributions to UK DB schemes were capped at 15 per cent of earnings. Combined employer and employee contributions to DC schemes were limited to £3,600 or an age-related proportion of earnings between 17.5 and 40 per cent, whichever was the greater. See also **Tax expenditure**.

Earnings-related benefits: pension benefits the value of which depend upon a person's pre-retirement earnings. Earnings-related benefits are intended to provide retiring workers with a degree of income maintenance. Unlike schemes paying flat-rate benefits, those providing earnings-related benefits perpetuate labour market inequalities into old age, since the best-paid individuals also receive the highest pensions.

Earnings-related contributions: contributions to a pension scheme which constitute a fixed proportion of contributors' earnings, e.g. 10 per cent. Earnings-related contributions are normally a feature of schemes which provide earnings-related benefits. The UK's BSP is unusual in that contributions are earnings related but benefits are flat-rate.

Earnings up-rating: see **Indexation**.

Economic activity rate: see **Labour market participation rate**.

Effective replacement rate: the actual level of income replacement at retirement for individuals with different pre-retirement earnings provided by a pension scheme. A scheme which provides a level of income replacement at retirement equal to 50 per cent of average earnings will have an effective replacement rate of 41.7 per cent for someone whose pre-retirement earnings were 20 per cent above the average. For someone with pre-retirement earnings 20 per cent below the average, the effective replacement rate would be 62.5 per cent.

Effective retirement age: the age at which people typically retire, which may differ from a scheme's normal retirement age. A scheme's effective retirement age can be higher than its normal age of retirement, where there are incentives for workers to remain in employment beyond pensionable age. Where workers are permitted to take a pension early on grounds of ill health or in return for reduced benefits, the effective retirement age can be significantly lower than the normal pension age. See also **Early retirement**.

Eligible earnings: see **Pensionable earnings**.

Employee Retirement Income Security Act (ERISA): passed in 1974 following the collapse of several large firms, which left pensioners with nothing because their DB schemes were under-funded. ERISA sought to protect members of occupational schemes through the introduction of minimum funding requirements, the outlawing of unfunded schemes and the creation of the Pension Benefit Guarantee Corporation. The Act raised the cost of providing DB pensions, leading many employers to close their schemes and offer money purchase plans instead.

Employee's contributions: contributions to a pension scheme made by employees. The level of contributions may be the same for all employees, or vary to reflect different employee characteristics. Moreover, an employee's contributions may or may not be the same as those made on their behalf by their employer. See also **Employer's contributions**.

Employer's contributions: contributions to a pension scheme made by employers on behalf of their employees. From a worker's point of view, employer's contributions can be thought of as a form of deferred earnings. For the employer, they are a non-wage labour cost. Where contributions are made by workers and employers, the contribution rate is often higher for the employer than it is for the employee. Consequently, the employer's share of total contributions is frequently greater than that of the employee. In Britain it is fairly common for two-thirds of a worker's total pension contributions to be paid by the employer.

Employer's scheme: see **Occupational scheme**.

Enhanced annuities: see **Impaired life annuities**.

Enhancements: see **Augmentation**.

Equity release plan: an arrangement whereby householders pledge their home to an insurance company in return for a stream of regular payments for the remainder of their life. Householders are able to continue living in their homes, which only become the property of the plan provider when they die. Equity release plans are thus a means by which elderly people can keep their homes while converting the equity in these properties into a retirement income. The level of income that can be obtained depends, among other things, on the value of the property and the householder's age and life expectancy when the plan commences.

Escalating annuity: see **Annuity**.

Expenditure tax: a tax regime which taxes income when it is consumed rather than when it is received. Because investment returns are not taxed until the savings on which they are earned are consumed, the post-tax return to saving equals the pre-tax return. Thus an expenditure tax is neutral with respect to saving. The value of consumption in the future is the same as current consumption. An expenditure tax is, therefore, widely believed to be the most appropriate regime for the taxation of pension savings.

External annuitants: individuals who purchase an annuity from a different insurance company from the one that managed their pension scheme's accumulation phase. They make up a relatively small proportion of the total annuity market in the UK and typically have larger than average terminal funds. See also **Open Market option**.

FAS 87: shorthand for Statement of Financial Accounting Standards No. 87, Employers Accounting for Pensions, issued by the US Financial Accounting Standards Board in December 1985. FASB 87 requires that where a deficit exists in an occupational DB pension scheme it must be shown in the sponsoring firm's company accounts. See also **FRS 17**.

Final salary scheme: a DB scheme which provides pension benefits the value of which depend upon a worker's earnings at or near to retirement. Final salary schemes provide individuals with deferred pension rights with retirement benefits linked to their salaries at or near the time they ceased to make contributions. See also **Defined Benefit Scheme**.

Financial Reporting Standard 17 (FRS 17): An accounting standard, published in November 2000, which requires UK firms to account for the financial positions of their DB pension schemes by reporting surpluses or deficits as assets or liabilities on their balance sheets. FRS 17 was not scheduled for full implementation until 2003. Even so, its publication appears to have sparked a rash of DB scheme closures by firms worried about its financial implications. Unlike SSAP 24, which it replaces, FRS 17 values pension scheme assets at current market prices, which, in the case of historically high-yielding equities, can be very volatile. Consequently, to avoid balance-sheet instability for sponsoring firms, schemes would need to invest more heavily in lower-yielding assets with less volatile prices. To make up for lower investment returns, sponsors would have to pay more into their schemes. Responding to sponsors' concerns, the ASB postponed full implementation of FRS 17 for a year, to give firms more time to adjust to the new accounting regime.

Financial Services Authority (FSA): the UK regulatory agency responsible, among other things, for the supervision of individual DC pension providers. The FSA is an independent body which derives its powers from the Financial Services and Markets Act of 2000. It is financed from a levy on financial services companies, and has a board of 15 appointed members including a Chairman, a Chief Executive Officer and two Managing Directors. Prior to the creation of the FSA, responsibility for the supervision of individual DC pension schemes lay with the Department for Trade and Industry.

Flat-rate benefits: pension benefits which are fixed in nominal terms and are unrelated to an individual's pre-retirement earnings. Schemes which provide flat-rate benefits, such as the UK's BSP, aim to provide workers with only a basic level of retirement income. Because benefits are the same for everyone, schemes paying flat-rate benefits provide a level of income replacement at retirement that differs between individuals according to their pre-retirement earnings.

Flat-rate contributions: contributions to a pension scheme which are the same for everyone irrespective of their earnings, e.g. £50 per month. Schemes with flat-rate contributions are regressive. It is more expensive for the poor to accrue pension benefits than it is for the rich, since contributions represent a larger proportion of the incomes of low earners.

Flexible annuity: an annuity contract which, in contrast to a level annuity, provides a stream of benefits which can vary over time. The nominal value of payments from a flexible annuity may be increased periodically according to a predetermined formula. Alternatively, payments may be linked to the value of assets in an investment fund such as a unit trust. Flexible annuities can be used to provide inflation-proofed pensions and/or to permit retirees to benefit from rising asset values.

Free-Standing Additional Voluntary Contributions (FSAVCs): additional voluntary contributions to an occupational scheme invested in an alternative fund to that nominated by the scheme's administrators. FSAVCs are particularly useful to workers who change jobs frequently, since they are more portable than normal AVCs. See also **Additional Voluntary Contributions; Portability**.

Front-loading: a feature of money purchase schemes where, because of the compounding of investment returns, early contributions are more valuable than those made later on.

Frozen pension: see **Deferred pensioners**.

Fuller (Ida May): worked as a legal secretary in Ludlow, Vermont. She is famed for being the first American to receive a social security pension. Having paid just $22 in contributions, Ida May, who died in 1975 aged 100, received pension benefits worth $23,000. She is frequently cited as an example of how immature unfunded pension schemes, combined with rapidly growing populations, permit successive generations of pensioners to receive in benefits much more than they paid in contributions.

Funded scheme (prefunded scheme): a pension scheme where active members make contributions to a fund, which is invested for growth and used to provide them with an annuity at retirement. Unlike contributors to PAYG schemes, those who contribute to funded schemes pay for their own pensions rather than paying somebody else's pension.

Funding rate: the amount of money, expressed as a proportion of earnings, that must be contributed by, or on behalf of, the active members of a DB scheme in order to provide them at retirement with the benefits to which they are entitled. A scheme's funding rate will depend, among other things, on the rate at which benefit entitlements accrue to members and upon the investment returns available. Anything that raises a scheme's benefit costs – increased longevity, for example – will increase its funding rate. With DC schemes, the funding rate is the proportion of earnings that must be contributed in order to achieve a particular pension income in retirement. The major determinants of DC scheme funding rates are the level of investment returns – net of taxes and charges – and expected annuity rates.

Funding rule: a statutory requirement for funded DB schemes to maintain a particular ratio of assets to liabilities, e.g 95 per cent, in order to ensure their solvency. Temporary deviations may be permitted to allow for fluctuations in asset prices. The funding rule for UK occupational DB schemes is the minimum funding requirement, introduced in the mid-1990s in response to the Maxwell affair. See also **Scheme-specific funding standards; Solvency**.

Generational accounting: a technique for estimating the tax burden for future generations arising from current fiscal policy. It relies on the fact that those alive in one time period can bequeath debts to future taxpayers in the form of un-repaid government borrowing. It involves a comparison of the generational accounts – taxes paid minus benefits received, expressed as a proportion of lifetime earnings – of successive population cohorts, in order to determine the extent to which overspending by one generation increases the tax burden on the next. Generational accounting has been used widely to estimate the costs that existing public pension and healthcare arrangements will create for future taxpayers due to population ageing.

Gerontology: The scientific study of ageing and its associated processes and problems. Gerontologists are interested in explaining and analysing the social, economic and cultural causes and consequences of ageing as well as its physical and psychological aspects.

Gompertz (Benjamin, 1779–1865): a pioneer of actuarial science and the originator of Gompertz's law of mortality. This law states that mortality rates increase geometrically with age. Gompertz found that the probability that an adult would die doubled with every additional eight years of life. He was a Fellow of the Royal Society and actuary and head clerk of the Alliance Assurance Company.

Goode Committee (Pension Law Review Committee): a committee, headed by Professor Roy Goode, established in response to the Maxwell affair to review the legal and regulatory framework for UK occupational pension schemes. In its report of September 1993, the Committee recommended, among other things, that one-third of the trustees of DC schemes and two-thirds of the trustees of DB schemes should be elected by scheme members. It also recommended the establishment of a compensation scheme for the victims of pensions crime and that minimum solvency rules for DB schemes should be introduced. The recommendations of the Goode Committee were, with some modifications, incorporated into the 1995 Pensions Act. See also **Minimum Funding Requirement**.

Government Actuary's Department (GAD): one of the Chancellor of the Exchequer's departments. The GAD consists of two directorates. One provides actuarial services to public sector organisations, including the valuation of pension scheme assets and liabilities and giving advice on funding rates, privatisation terms, etc. The other directorate provides advice on social security arrangements in the UK and some other countries, as well as advising on private pensions policy and regulation. It also carries out periodic pension scheme surveys and produces the UK's official population projections. The post of Government Actuary evolved from the appointment of Sir Alfred Watson as Chief Actuary to the National Health Insurance Joint Committee, in 1912, and the GAD was created in 1919. It is unusual in that it is both a department of the UK Government and a commercial actuarial consultancy.

Graduated Pension Scheme (GPS): the forerunner of SERPS. Introduced in 1961, the Graduated Pension Scheme was an earnings-related supplementary state pension. In return for additional National Insurance contributions, graduated according to income, workers could build up entitlements to an earnings-related top-up to the basic state pension. In 1971 the Government proposed scrapping the GPS, which was ultimately replaced with SERPS in 1975. Though short-lived, the GPS established the first formal link between state and private pension provision in the UK. A worker could opt out of the GPS if his or her employer provided an occupational scheme offering equivalent or better benefits – a process known as non-participation.

Graunt (John, 1620–1674): the creator of the field of medical epidemiology and an early pioneer of actuarial science and statistics. A London businessman, Graunt carried out a detailed mathematical analysis on decades of mortality data (the bills of mortality) for England and Wales, the results of which he published in 1662. He was the first person to construct a life table by using data on human mortality to project survival rates. In recognition of his achievements, Graunt became the first non-scientist ever to be appointed to the Royal Academy.

Group Personal Pension: a single arrangement for collecting PPP contributions from a group of individuals such as the employees of a particular firm.

Guaranteed annuity: an annuity which guarantees to pay out for a fixed period – usually 5 or 10 years – whether or not the annuitant lives. Guaranteed annuities sometimes provide for full or partial commutation of remaining income in the event of the annuitant's death.

Guaranteed Minimum Contribution (GMC): the minimum amount that must be contributed to a contracted-out occupational DC scheme, equal to the National Insurance rebate to APPs.

Guaranteed Minimum Pension (GMP): the minimum pension that must be provided by a contracted-out DB occupational scheme in the UK in respect of service prior to 6 April 1997. The GMP ensured that those who contracted out of SERPS would receive an occupational pension at least as good as they could have got from the state supplementary scheme. For service after 6 April 1997, the GMP is replaced with an obligation for schemes to provide price indexation for workers' accrued pension rights up to a maximum of 5 per cent.

Home Responsibilities Protection (HRP): National Insurance credits for those who have temporarily left the labour force in order to bring up children or care for an elderly or disabled relative. HRP effectively reduces the number of years of National Insurance contributions required for a full basic state pension. It also entitles people to receive £1 per week of pension income from the second state pension for each year in which they have received HRP. HRP is only available to those claiming child benefit or income support. The overwhelming majority of HRP recipients are women.

Immediate annuity: see **Purchased life annuity**.

Impaired life annuities (enhanced annuities): annuities providing rate enhancements to those with a diminished life expectancy. See also **Annuity rate**.

Income drawdown plan: an arrangement made possible by the Finance Act of 1995, whereby UK individual pension plan holders aged between 50 and 75 may draw part of their accumulated funds each year as income. The minimum and maximum amounts that may be drawn down annually are set by the government, with these limits being reviewed every three years. Individuals have the option to annuitise their remaining funds at any time up to age 75, when annuitisation becomes compulsory. Income drawdown makes it possible for individuals to obtain better annuity rates by deferring annuitisation until they are older, but to receive an amount of retirement income in the meantime.

Income replacement rate: see **Replacement rate**.

Indexation (uprating): the practice of linking increases in pension payments – or the value of accrued pension rights – to changes in an index of prices or earnings. By increasing pensions in line with prices (price uprating), their real value is preserved. Earnings uprating (the linking of pension increases to changes in earned incomes) will lead to an increase in the real value of pension payments and maintain their value relative to earned incomes, because earnings tend to rise faster than prices. Prior to 1979, the UK's basic old age pension was indexed to the annual increase in prices or earnings, whichever was the higher. Since then, the basic state pension has been uprated solely in line with prices. Consequently, its value has declined, and will continue to decline, relative to average earnings. See also **Limited price indexation**.

Indexed annuity: see **Annuity**.

Indexed Benefit Obligation (IBO): a measure of the value of an ongoing DB scheme's future liabilities, which assumes that preserved pensions are indexed to earnings and that pensions in payment are indexed to prices or earnings. See also **Accumulated Benefit Obligation**.

Index-linked benefits: retirement benefits that are uprated annually in line with changes in some reference index. See also **Indexation**.

Index tracker fund (passive fund): an investment fund set up to achieve returns that match the performance of some index of financial assets such as the UK's FTSE 100. Instead of actively trading their assets in order to profit from changes in their market prices, index tracker funds adopt a passive 'buy and hold' strategy. Their investments are allocated to different assets in proportions that mirror their representations in the indices being tracked. Thus, the returns achieved by an index tracker fund will replicate those earned on the particular index it is tracking. Pension schemes that are run as index tracker funds have low charges compared with those that are actively managed, because their brokerage costs are lower.

Individual Retirement Account (IRA): the American equivalent of a British personal pension plan. IRAs were introduced in 1974, for employees who lacked access to an occupational scheme. In 1981, they were made available to all workers and their families.

Induced retirement effect: refers to the way in which improvements in pension scheme generosity influence peoples' lifetime labour supply decisions. An improvement in scheme generosity will induce some individuals to retire earlier than they would otherwise have done by permitting them to obtain a target level of nominal retirement income with fewer years of contributions. Because an improvement in scheme generosity raises the opportunity cost of early retirement, other individuals will be induced to retire later than they would have done in the absence of any increase. The net effect of an increase in scheme generosity on aggregate labour supply will, therefore, depend upon the relative size of these two groups of workers.

Infant mortality rate: the number of deaths among children aged nought to one per thousand live births in a year. In Japan, for example, there were 5,062 infant deaths in the year 2000, and 1,265,500 live births. The infant mortality rate was thus 5,062 divided by 1,265,500 times 1,000, which equals 4. Infant mortality rates for Canada, America and the UK in the same year were respectively 5, 7 and 6. Less developed countries tend to have much higher rates of infant mortality.

Inflation: an increase, over time, in the average price of goods and services, measured in the UK by changes in the retail price index. Because inflation reduces the purchasing power of money, pension benefits must be increased in line with increases in prices if their real value is to be maintained. See also **Limited price indexation**.

Insured pension scheme: a scheme which provides a pension via an insurance policy. In the UK, the majority of small occupational schemes and all individual pension plans are insured schemes.

Integration: the process whereby some UK DB occupational schemes incorporate part or all of the value of the basic old age pension in their calculation of benefit levels.

Intergenerational redistribution: the transfer of income from one generation to another. Intergenerational redistribution is a feature of all pension schemes. PAYG schemes are explicitly intergenerationally redistributive, because income is transferred directly from workers to pensioners in the form of taxes and benefits. With funded schemes, retirees use their accumulated funds to purchase a claim on part of the wealth created by the economically active population.

Internal annuitants: individuals who purchase an annuity from the same insurance company that managed their pension scheme's accumulation phase. They make up the largest proportion of the total annuity market in the UK. See also **Open market option**.

Intragenerational redistribution: the transfer of income between members of the same generation. Intragenerational redistribution is a significant feature of funded DB pension schemes, because early leavers can end up subsidising the pensions of long-stayers. Any investment returns on the assets of early leavers with preserved pensions – above those required for indexation purposes – represent a subsidy to other workers who remain as active scheme members. Intragenerational redistribution is also an important feature of DC pensions via the annuity market. See also **Mortality cross-subsidy**.

Labour force: see **Workforce**.

Labour market participation rate (economic activity rate): the number of employed and self-employed people in a population expressed as a proportion of all individuals of working age. Participation will always be less than 100 per cent, because some people are unable to work due to sickness or disability, some are unable to find employment and others do not need to work. Total labour market participation in Britain stood at 63.1 per cent during May–July 2003. For males the figure was 71.1 per cent, compared with 55.6 per cent for females. Other things being equal, the lower the total labour market participation rate the higher public pension contributions will need to be, since only economically active individuals make pension contributions.

Level annuity: see **Annuity**.

Liabilities: the financial obligations of a pension scheme to its beneficiaries. With DC schemes, liabilities are limited to the value of contributors' accumulated funds. DB schemes have a more complex liability structure comprising short-term and long-term liabilities. In the short term, DB schemes must pay the benefits to which current pensioners are entitled. Over the longer term, they must raise the value of pensions in payment in accordance with the indexation rules and meet their benefit obligations to contributing members and those with deferred pensions.

Life expectancy: the number of years a typical member of a population can be expected to live. Life expectancy has risen in developed countries by around two years every decade since the 1960s, due to factors such as medical advances, improved health awareness, rising incomes, and better standards of health and safety in the workplace. See also **Age-specific life expectancy**.

Life table: a statistical table prepared by an actuary showing estimates of the probabilities of individuals of different ages surviving for a given period of time, e.g. one year or five years. Life tables thus allow estimates of life expectancy to be made for individuals of all ages. Because men and women have different mortality characteristics, life tables are prepared separately for each sex. Among other things, life tables are used by insurance companies to set life assurance premiums and annuity rates, and by national governments to forecast future public pension expenditures.

Limited Price Indexation (LPI): the obligation on providers of DB occupational schemes to uprate deferred pensions in line with inflation, up to a maximum of 5 per cent. LPI means that in years when inflation is above 5 per cent, workers with deferred pensions will see the real value of their entitlements eroded.

Linkage: the extent to which pension benefits vary in line with contributions. Where linkage is strong, as in a pure social insurance scheme, those who contribute the most during their working life receive the highest pensions. With flat-rate schemes, such as Britain's basic state pension, linkage is weak, because all individuals who qualify for a full pension receive the same amounts regardless of how much they contribute.

Longevity risk: the risk that retired individuals might live longer than they anticipate and so consume all their savings before they die. By annuitising their savings at retirement, individuals can insure against longevity risk. See also **Annuitisation**.

Lower Earnings Limit (LEL): the threshold level of earnings above which UK National Insurance contributions become payable. On 6 April 2002, the LEL stood at £4,628 a year – £89 per week. The LEL is normally increased annually in line with inflation, although in his 2002 budget the Chancellor of the Exchequer announced his intention to freeze this threshold in 2003–2004. See also **Upper Earnings Limit**.

Managed fund: see **Actively managed fund**.

Management slack: inefficiency in the fund management process which results in reduced returns to pension scheme members. Management slack arises where, because of a lack of competition amongst those managing pension funds, managers have an incentive to pursue their own interests rather than seeking to maximise the returns to scheme members. The interests of both parties can be allied through, for example, linking manager's remuneration to fund performance. This, however, would expose members to the risk of losses arising from excessive risk taking by managers. See also **Moral hazard**.

Market risk: the potential for adverse asset and/or annuity market conditions at the time DC pensions are taken to result in low levels of retirement income. One way for DC plan-holders to protect themselves against a fall in equity prices is (where plan rules permit) to trade potential growth for stability by shifting their funds into lower-yielding but less volatile assets such as government bonds. Income drawdown can sometimes be used to obtain a retirement income without the need to annuitise the funds in a DC plan when annuity rates are low.

Married Women's Rate (MWR): a reduced rate of National Insurance contributions which married women could opt to pay prior to 1978. Married women making these lower-rate contributions forfeit their entitlement to a state pension in their own right. Although the option to make lower-rate contributions was withdrawn in 1978, those already contributing at the MWR were permitted to continue doing so. Around 700,000 married women were making MWR contributions in the early 1990s.

Mature scheme: a DB pension scheme the membership of which comprises a high proportion of pensioners with full benefit entitlements. Mature funded schemes have large immediate liabilities relative to total contributions. Because inflows to and outflows from PAYG schemes must be equal if they are self-financing, total contributions must rise as these schemes mature.

Means test: a test of income and/or wealth used to determine a person's eligibility to receive a particular benefit. Benefits are denied either wholly or in part to individuals whose incomes and/or wealth is above some cut-off level. Means testing is used extensively in the UK to limit the cost of providing retirees with non-pension welfare benefits by targeting benefit payments on those who need them most. Such tests may, however, discourage those in need of benefits from applying for them if the means test is excessively complex or intrusive.

Member Nominated Trustee (MNT): a member of the trustee board of a UK occupational pension scheme who is elected by the scheme members. The presence of MNTs on trustee boards – like the presence of member trustees – gives beneficiaries representation in the running of their scheme. Since 1997, at least one-third of the members of trustee boards must be elected by scheme members.

Members (beneficiaries): individuals who are entitled to receive benefits from a pension scheme. These include those currently in receipt of a pension, the scheme's current contributors, and individuals who have a pension entitlement but have ceased contributing. See also **Preserved pension rights**.

Minimum Funding Requirement (MFR): a standard measure of solvency for UK DB occupational pension schemes, introduced in the aftermath of the Maxwell affair. The MFR places a legal requirement upon DB schemes to hold assets the market value of which would be sufficient to cover their pension liabilities if they were to be wound up immediately. Schemes with deficits of up to 10 per cent are allowed five years in which to return to full solvency. Where a deficit is greater than 10 per cent, a return to 90 per cent solvency must be achieved within one year. Critics of the MFR claim that the solvency standard, which was meant to protect pension scheme members, has increased sponsors' costs and been a factor in the closure of numerous schemes. In 2001, the government announced that the MFR was to be scrapped and replaced with scheme-specific funding standards.

Minimum Income Guarantee (MIG): a top-up social security benefit for pensioners whose incomes fall below a minimum level, guaranteed by the government. In April 2003, the MIG was set at £102.10 per week for a single person and £155.80 for a couple. When it was introduced, in April 1999, the government announced its intention to uprate the MIG in line with increases in earnings. This contrasts with price indexation, the method used to uprate the basic state pension. As with all means-tested benefits, the effectiveness of the MIG at reducing pensioner poverty depends upon take-up.

Money purchase scheme: see **Defined Contribution scheme**.

Money's worth ratio: a measure of the value for money to different individuals of contributing to a public pension scheme. It is calculated as the ratio of the present value of expected pension payments to the present value of employee and employer contributions. A money's worth ratio that is greater than 1 implies that contributing to the public pension scheme is worthwhile. On the other hand, a ratio of less than 1 does not necessarily mean that contributing to the scheme is not worthwhile. Public schemes provide longevity insurance and inflation-proofing, benefits that are not measured but may be valued very highly by some individuals. Money's worth ratios can also be used to measure the value for money of private annuities, calculated as the ratio of the present value of the expected income stream to the purchase price.

Moral hazard: a situation where, because their behaviour cannot be properly monitored or controlled, an insured party can alter the risk borne by the insurer. For example, a smoker who is able to purchase an annuity from an insurance company on superior terms to a non-smoker, because of their shorter life expectancy, may subsequently quit smoking and live longer as a result. Similarly, where workers' accrued pension rights are protected by benefit insurance, they may encourage their fund managers to take excessive investment risks, thereby making an insurance payout more likely.

Mortality cross-subsidy: a device employed by private annuity providers whereby the funds contributed by annuitants who die early are used to gear up the incomes of those with longer lives.

Mortality drag: sometimes called the annuity premium, this is the income provided by annuities above the returns earned on the assets used to back them. See also **Mortality cross-subsidy**.

Mortality rate: a measure of the number of deaths occurring annually in a population or sub-group of a population. See also **Death rate; Infant mortality rate**.

Mortality substitution: the term used to denote the way in which the killer conditions of later life (cancer, heart disease, strokes, etc.) have, in the developed world, become responsible for the majority of deaths each year in place of the fatal illnesses of childhood. Mortality substitution is contributing to population ageing, because large numbers of individuals who would have succumbed to the killer diseases of childhood and early adult life (measles, diphtheria, whooping cough, tuberculosis, etc.) are now living well into old age. It is the result of, among other things, mass immunisation programmes, better nutrition, improvements in housing, and advances in neonatal and paediatric medicine.

Myners Report: a report on institutional investment by the Myners Committee, chaired by Paul Myners, the chairman of Gartmore Investment Management, published in 2001. As well as recommending that trustees of UK occupational pension schemes should be paid, and receive appropriate training, Myners recommended the scrapping of the MFR and its replacement with scheme-specific funding standards.

National Insurance Contributions (NICs): compulsory social security contributions made by UK individuals and their employees which earn entitlement to a variety of welfare benefits, including healthcare and state pension payments. Employee NICs are currently levied at a rate of 11 per cent on earned incomes between an upper and a lower earnings limit. They are also payable at a rate of 1 per cent on earnings above the UEL. There is no UEL for employer NICs, which are payable on employees' incomes above the LEL.

National Insurance fund: the revenues collected each year from UK National Insurance contributions. The term is a misnomer, since NICs do not accumulate in a fund. Instead, NICs are used to finance Britain's National Health Service and public pension schemes as they are received.

National Pensions Reserve Fund (NPRF): a fund established by the Irish government in April 2001 to help finance future public pension expenditures. The fund is accumulated from tax revenues and will not begin to contribute to public pension expenditures until at least 2025. It is administered by a seven-member NPRF Commission, which must pursue a strictly commercial investment strategy. Unlike the US OASDI trust fund, which invests in American government securities, the NPRF is not permitted to invest in Irish government bonds.

Non-contributory pension scheme: a scheme which provides workers with a pension at retirement without the requirement for them or their employers to make financial contributions. Eligibility for a pension is usually determined on the basis of years of residence in the case of public schemes, or length of service, in the case of occupational schemes. The benefits provided tend to be rather low and, in the case of public schemes, are often means-tested.

Non-pensionable employment: either employment which does not provide employees with access to a pension scheme, or a period of employment during which an employee was not a member of an occupational pension scheme.

Normal retirement age: the age at which employees in particular occupations normally retire or might reasonably be expected to retire. In many occupations the normal retirement age is often some way below the official retirement age due, for example, to high levels of early retirement on grounds of ill health.

Notional Defined Contribution (NDC) scheme: a PAYG-financed DB scheme which pays retirement benefits linked to the amounts contributed by individuals, rather than to the earnings on which contributions were made. Contributions are assumed to earn a certain rate of return in order to generate a notional retirement fund. Benefits take the form of indexed annuities, with annuity rates that are actuarially fair between cohorts with different life expectancies. An NDC scheme has recently been established in Sweden.

Occupational Pensions Board (OPB): the forerunner to the Occupational Pensions Regulatory Authority (OPRA). It came into existence in 1973, and was wound up in April 1997. The Board operated the certification procedures for contracting out of SERPs and was responsible for supervising the administration and financial soundness of contracted-out occupational and personal pension schemes. The Board also authorised the modification of scheme rules and scheme wind ups, and advised the Secretary of State on regulatory matters. An overhaul of the regulatory and supervisory arrangements for occupational schemes, in the aftermath of the Maxwell affair, led to the winding up of the OPB and the creation of OPRA. See also **Occupational Pensions Regulatory Authority**.

Occupational Pensions Regulatory Authority (OPRA): the agency responsible for the supervision of UK DB occupational pension schemes since 1997, when it superseded the OPB. It is comprised of 7 government-appointed members and a staff of around 200. Where problems are brought to its attention – it relies on whistle-blowers rather than the routine inspection of scheme documentation – it has the power to appoint and dismiss trustees, levy fines on sponsors and trustees, and require schemes to be wound up.

Occupational scheme (employer's scheme): a pension scheme sponsored by an employer, the membership of which is restricted to current and former employees of the sponsoring firm. Occupational schemes may be of the DB or the DC type and may be financed on a PAYG or a funded basis. In Britain and the US, employers provide occupational schemes, and workers join them, on a voluntary basis, whereas in some other countries (Australia, for example) occupational pensions are mandatory for both employers and employees. Although membership of UK occupational schemes has been in decline since the 1980s, nearly half of all workers in Britain are members of an employer's scheme.

Old-age dependency rate (old-age dependency ratio): the ratio of old to working-age people in a population. It is calculated as the number of old people divided by the number of individuals of working age multiplied by 100. The value of the old-age dependency rate will depend upon the age range chosen for workers and the threshhold at which old age begins. For example, this book defines the workforce as comprising individuals aged between 20 and 59, and the elderly as those aged 60 and over. Sometimes, though, the workforce is defined as comprising individuals aged 20 to 64, with old age taken to begin at 65. The old-age dependency ratios for Britain in 2000, based upon the two different approaches, are 37.83 and 26.52 respectively.

Open market option: the right, in the UK, for contributors to individual pension schemes to purchase an annuity from a different insurance company from the one that managed their plan's accumulation phase.

Only a small proportion of annuitants (less than 20 per cent) exercise their open market option to shop around and get the best available annuity rates. Those who do tend to have larger than average terminal funds. This is not surprising, since insurance companies typically set a relatively high minimum premium for external annuitants. The open market option, therefore, is of little value to low income groups, since they tend to have relatively small funds to annuitise.

Over-annuitisation: saving more for retirement, because pension contributions are compulsory, than would be saved voluntarily. Over-annuitisation may be desirable where, because they are feckless or myopic, workers would fail to save enough voluntarily to ensure that they had sufficient resources to see them through retirement. If, on the other hand, people are forced to save more than they need for retirement, their lifetime consumption will be lower than it needs to be.

Over-funded scheme (scheme surplus): a situation where, as a result of an actuarial valuation, a funded DB scheme is found to hold assets the value of which exceeds its liabilities. A scheme can become over-funded due to an increase in the market value of the assets it holds or the returns they yield, a fall in the value of its liabilities, or if contributions are too high. A degree of over-funding may be desirable to protect schemes from adverse movements in the value of their assets and liabilities. In Britain, sponsors of schemes with large surpluses are given a limited time in which to reduce the level of over-funding to 105 per cent of liabilities. This may be achieved through a benefit increase, a reduction or temporary suspension of contributions, or by payment of part of the surplus to the sponsor. In Britain, a scheme surplus is deemed to be the property of the sponsor.

Participation: see **Take-up**.

Passive fund: see **Index tracker fund**.

Passivity ratio: the ratio of years of working life to years of retirement. In Europe and elsewhere passivity ratios have been falling, due to increasing longevity and reductions in effective retirement ages. In the European Union countries they averaged four, in the 1960s, compared with less than three in 2000. The passivity ratio is significant because, when multiplied by the rate of return on financial assets, it gives a measure of the returns to funded pensions. To stabilise the passivity ratio, the effective retirement age would need to rise in line with increases in life expectancy.

Pay-As-You-Go (PAYG): a method of financing a pension scheme whereby pension payments are made directly from the contributions of workers. Although the amount contributed need not be the same for all workers, for a PAYG scheme to be solvent, the total value of contributions must be sufficient to meet the benefit claims of pensioners and cover the scheme's administration costs. The average level of contribution required for solvency can be calculated as $C = PB/N$, where C is the average amount that must be contributed, P the number of pensioners, B the average value of pension benefits and N the number of contributing workers. Thus, an increase in the ratio of pensioners to workers and/or a rise in average pension benefits will raise the level of contributions required to maintain scheme solvency. The vast majority of public pension schemes, and some occupational schemes, are financed on a PAYG basis. See also **Book reserve scheme; Population ageing; Public pension scheme**.

Pension: a regular income received for life by a retired person in place of earnings from employment. Pension payments may be earnings related, being a specific fraction of an individual's prior earnings from employment, or flat rate – a fixed weekly or monthly amount unrelated to previous earnings. They may also be fixed for life, or periodically increased in line with increases in some variable such as average earnings or prices. Although pensions are usually derived from membership of a pension scheme, they are sometimes awarded by an employer as a gratuity for long or exceptional service.

Pensionable earnings (eligible earnings): the portion of a worker's earnings which is used to calculate his or her pension benefits and on which pension contributions are made. Individuals' pensionable earnings are frequently less than their total earnings. For example, contributions to Britain's two public pension schemes are only payable on earnings between a lower and an upper limit. In addition, many private schemes do not count elements of earned income like overtime, bonus payments and meal allowances as pensionable earnings.

Pensionable employment: either employment where a worker has the right to join a pension scheme – whether or not he or she actually joins – or the period of employment during which an individual was a member of an occupational pension scheme.

Pensionable service: the period during which a worker was an active member of an employer's DB pension scheme, and on the basis of which pension benefits are payable. See also **Qualifying service**.

Pension age: see **Retirement age**.

Pension Benefit Guarantee Corporation (PBGC): established in 1974 to provide a level of benefit insurance for members of US occupational DB schemes where the sponsoring employer becomes bankrupt. It is financed from premiums paid by the sponsors of the schemes it insures and from the returns on its own investments. Premiums are lower for well-funded schemes, giving sponsors an incentive to maintain adequate funding levels. Similar insurance arrangements exist for members of employer-provided schemes in Germany and Sweden.

Pension Commission: a Commission charged with reporting regularly to Britain's Secretary of State for Work and Pensions on whether there is a need to move beyond the UK's current voluntarist approach to private pension saving. The Commission, which was established in 2003, comprises three Commissioners and a secretariat. Its first 'full report' is expected to be published sometime in 2005, following an interim report in mid-2004.

Pensioner: an individual currently in receipt of a pension. Three main groups of pensioners can be identified: state pensioners, who receive public pensions; occupational pensioners, receiving pensions from previous employers; and those who are drawing a pension from a personal pension plan. These groups are not mutually exclusive. Pensioners frequently fall into all three groups, deriving their total pension incomes from a combination of public, occupational and personal pensions.

Pensioner household: a household which contains at least one person at or above state pension age.

Pensioner unit: either a single person in receipt of a state pension, or a couple – married or cohabiting – where the man is over state pension age, even if the woman is not. Couples where only the woman is receiving a state pension are not counted as pensioner units.

Pension forecast: a forecast of how much a worker can expect to receive at retirement from Britain's state pension schemes on the basis of their contribution record to date. In 1998, the government announced its ambition to introduce integrated forecasts, which would indicate a worker's overall pension position – public as well as private. Collecting and processing the information required to produce these forecasts would be extremely expensive. It is perhaps not surprising, then, that this idea appears to have been quietly dropped.

Pension Law Review Committee: see **Goode Committee**.

Pension lump sum: a once-and-for-all cash benefit from a pension scheme received at retirement in addition to an annuity. In the UK, 25 per cent of the terminal fund in a money purchase scheme may be taken as a lump sum. The value of lump sums payable from DB plans varies between schemes, but is usually calculated as a fixed fraction of a worker's final salary multiplied by years of pensionable service.

Pension plan: see **Pension scheme**.

Pension Protection Fund (PPF): a compulsory insurance scheme for UK occupational DB schemes, to be introduced in April 2005 and similar to the US Pension Benefit Guarantee Corporation. The PPF, which will be financed from the premiums paid by insured schemes, is expected to guarantee 90 per cent of members' benefits – up to a maximum of around £50,000 a year – should their scheme's sponsoring employer become insolvent. Premiums will be paid in the form of a double levy, consisting of a flat-rate charge per member and a risk-adjusted charge linked to a scheme's funding level. The aim of the risk-adjusted component is to provide sponsors with an incentive to maintain adequate levels of funding and to ensure that 'good' schemes don't end up cross-subsidising 'bad' schemes.

Pensions burden: the annual cost of providing public pension benefits expressed as a proportion of a country's national income. The pensions burden tends to be comparatively large in countries where public pension benefits are high relative to earned incomes, e.g. in Germany and Italy where it is over 10 per cent. In Britain, where public pension payments are low compared with incomes from employment, the pensions burden is less than 5 per cent. See also **Transfer ratio**.

Pension scheme (pension plan): a mechanism for providing retired people with a pension, and for allowing those of working age to build up entitlements to a pension when they retire. Although some schemes are non-contributory, most provide pensions in return for contributions made during a person's working life. Pension schemes can be organised by governments, employers or commercial pension providers. Membership may be voluntary, although it is often compulsory. In countries like Britain and the United States, a variety of different schemes operate alongside each other. In other countries – Italy, for example – the range of schemes is more restricted.

Pension system (retirement income system): the arrangements in a country for providing retiring workers with incomes to replace their earnings from employment. Comparisons of pension systems are often made with reference to the relative importance to pensioners of income from different tiers of provision. Three tiers are usually identified: the first or bottom tier, comprising PAYG public pension schemes and old-age welfare benefits financed from general taxation; the second or middle tier, consisting of occupational schemes; and the third or top tier which comprises individual pensions and other forms of private retirement income. Reducing the proportion of pensioners' incomes that comes from the first tier, and increasing the shares coming from the second and third tiers, is a major element in pension reform around the world.

Persistency: the extent to which purchasers of private pensions, insurance policies, endowment plans etc. stick with these products rather than allowing them to lapse prematurely. Persistency is likely to be highest for products where discontinuance carries a financial penalty. Among the many reasons why private pensions such as PPPs and stakeholder plans may be allowed to lapse are the inability of the purchaser to continue making contributions, dissatisfaction with the investment performance of these plans, or because people have come to regard their purchases of these products as a mistake. Persistency can also fall when new products are introduced which offer superior terms. The persistency of PPPs fell when stakeholder plans were introduced as a cheap and flexible alternative to these products.

Personal Pension Plan (PPP): an individual pension plan which became available to employees in the UK in 1988. PPPs became the subject of a notorious mis-selling scandal. Contributors to 'approved' PPPs can become entitled to pay NICs at a reduced rate by opting out of the earnings-related component of Britain's state pension arrangements. Contributors to PPPs must annuitise at least three-quarters of their accumulated funds between the ages of 50 and 75 and may take up to 25 per cent as a tax-free lump sum. High charges and rigid contribution schedules mean that PPPs are not an appropriate way for individuals with low to middle incomes to save for retirement. To remedy this situation, a variant of the PPP, the stakeholder pension, was introduced in 2001. As well as having lower charges and greater contribution flexibility, stakeholder pensions are available to everybody, not just those in paid employment.

Pickering Report: a report on the simplification of occupational pension provision in the UK by Alan Pickering, published on 11 July 2002. Pickering, a former chairman of the NAPF, had been commissioned by the government in September 2001 to conduct a review of pension provision in order to identify ways to encourage retirement saving by reducing the complexity of choice and regulation in Britain's pension arrangements. The Report contained more than 50 recommendations. These included raising the state pension age, replacing OPRA with a new kind of regulator, the abolition of vesting periods, removal of the obligation on contracted-out schemes for limited price indexation of pension benefits and lower accrual rates. To improve transparency and simplify choice, Pickering recommended that the number of different types of scheme in operation should be reduced from more than twenty to just two or three.

Political risk: the potential for pension benefits to be reduced and/or contribution rates to rise as a result of the politically motivated actions or inaction of governments. Although political risk is an inherent feature of public pension schemes because governments set benefit levels, contribution rates and retirement ages, it is also a feature of private pensions. Governments can alter the tax regime under which private schemes operate and place restrictions on their investment strategies. Public or private schemes may be placed in jeopardy, if governments are unwilling to take necessary but politically unpopular action to ensure their long-term viability.

Ponzi scheme: a pyramid investment scheme which relies on the income from successive groups of new investors to make payments to those who joined earlier. These schemes collapse when the income from the latest group of new investors is insufficient to cover payments to those who joined before. Ponzi schemes take their name from Charles Ponzi, an Italian immigrant to America, who in 1920 was able to rake in an estimated $15 million in just 8 months by persuading tens of thousands of Bostonians to join a pyramid investment scheme. PAYG pension schemes are sometimes characterised as Ponzi schemes, because each new generation of contributors must finance the pension payments of previous generations.

Population ageing: an increase, over time, in the average age of the population, leading to a rise in the ratio of old to young people. It is mainly the result of increasing longevity and falling birth rates. Population ageing has given rise to concerns about labour shortages, the affordability of pay-as-you-go public pension schemes and the cost of state-funded health care. While some commentators see population ageing as a desirable consequence of economic and social development, other, more alarmist, pundits argue that it will lead to social ossification and intergenerational conflict over scarce public resources. See also **Demographic transition; Old-age dependency ratio**.

Population projections: forecasts of the size and composition of future populations. A variety of methods can be used to construct them; some are relatively simple and others are rather complex. The principles, though, are always the same. An initial population is selected, about which a great deal is already known. Assumptions are then made about future rates of fertility, mortality and migration to forecast the way in which this 'base population' will evolve over time. The inclusion of assumptions about fertility, mortality and migration rates means that population projections are inherently uncertain. They are forecasts of what would happen on the basis of the assumptions made, not predictions of what will actually happen.

Portability: the term used to denote the ability of workers to move their accrued pension entitlements between occupational pension schemes when they change jobs. Complete portability requires that workers are able to make transfers between different employers' schemes without any loss of entitlement in the case of DB schemes, or any reduction in their fund's value in the case of DC plans. In practice, portability tends to be less than complete, due, for example, to the existence of vesting periods and transfer charges. Portability has implications for labour mobility within and between countries. Where portability is weak, workers will have a diminished incentive to move between employers. Consequently, national and international labour markets are likely to be more flexible where there is a high degree of portability.

Portability losses: losses which arise when workers move between pension schemes such that the value of the pension they ultimately receive is less than it would have been had they stayed in a single scheme. It has been shown that a single job change can result in a portability loss of up to 16 per cent, due, amongst other things, to differences in the way schemes calculate the cash values of accrued pension rights and service credits. Workers who experience six job changes can incur losses of between 25 and 30 per cent. Only workers who move between employers who are members of a transfer circuit are immune from portability losses.

Prefunded scheme: see **Funded scheme**.

Preserved pension rights: the accrued retirement benefits of occupational DB scheme members who have left the employment of the sponsoring firm which have not been transferred to another employer's scheme and will have to be paid at a future date. In the UK, preserved pensions must be uprated annually in line with inflation, up to a maximum of 5 per cent, to maintain their real value. See also **Early leavers**.

Price uprating: see **Indexation**.

Principal–agent problem: a problem of control that arises where one party (the principal) owns assets which it employs another party (the agent) to manage on its behalf. Agent may not act in the best interests of the principal if their actions cannot be properly monitored or controlled. In the case of funded pension schemes – where the principals are the scheme members, and fund managers their agents – lazy managers may pursue an investment strategy aimed at achieving a satisfactory return on the assets they manage rather than working hard to obtain the best possible return.

Prioritisation: the controversial requirement, introduced in the wake of the Maxwell affair, for existing pensioners to be given first claim on the assets of a DB occupational scheme when it is wound up. Although prioritisation was intended to safeguard the incomes of those with pensions in payment, it puts the pensions of current contributors in jeopardy. Following the winding up of an under funded scheme, there may be few, if any, assets remaining for current contributors once the interests of those with pensions in payment have been protected. Prioritisation is most problematic for workers who are close to retirement age, because they have relatively few years in which to make good any pension losses arising from the termination of an under-funded scheme. It also provides an incentive for members of schemes with a funding deficit to retire at the earliest opportunity, rather than remaining in employment.

Projected Benefit Obligation (PBO): a measure of an ongoing DB scheme's future liabilities which allows for increases in the value of workers' accrued benefits arising from future earnings growth.

Protected rights: the pension benefits from a contracted-out UK DC scheme which derive from guaranteed minimum payments or from guaranteed minimum contributions and the investment returns they earn. See also **Contracted-out scheme**.

Protected rights annuity: an annuity purchased from the protected rights portion of an individual's terminal fund in a UK DC pension scheme. The rates offered on protected rights annuities by insurance companies must be the same for men and women, even though women on average live longer than men and should, according to the principle of actuarial fairness, be offered lower rates.

Public pension scheme (state pension scheme): a pension scheme run by, or on behalf of, a national government. Most public schemes are DB pay-as-you-go schemes providing either flat-rate or earnings-related retirement benefits. Participation is usually compulsory for all workers covered by such schemes. Coverage may be restricted to a particular section of the workforce, or may include everyone in employment and self-employment. Projections of rapid population ageing in the coming decades have raised concerns about the long-term affordability of public pension schemes. In most developed countries, spending on the elderly, including expenditure on public pensions, absorbs a substantial proportion of GDP. Governments have, therefore, recently been introducing reforms aimed at limiting the financial impact of population ageing on their public schemes. Reforms include raising the state pension age, cutting pension benefits, providing incentives for individuals to join alternative private schemes (or compelling them to do so), and making increasing use of means testing. In America and Ireland, an element of prefunding has been introduced into public pensions. see also **Pay-As-You-Go; Population ageing; State pension age**.

Public service pension: a pension received by a retired public sector employee. Public service pensions may be paid from public service schemes, or they may constitute a special category of public pension. For example, until the mid-1990s, some groups of Italian public servants were permitted to retire with a full state pension much earlier than other workers.

Public service scheme: an occupational pension scheme for public sector employees, e.g. the UK's civil service scheme. Public service schemes sometimes provide superior retirement benefits and/or have lower retirement ages compared with equivalent schemes in the private sector.

Purchased life annuity (immediate annuity, voluntary annuity): an annuity which is purchased voluntarily rather than being bought under the compulsory annuitisation rules applying to UK DC plans. For tax purposes, payments from purchased life annuities are split into income and returns on capital.

Qualifying service: the minimum period of employment that must be served by an employee in order to become entitled to receive occupational pension benefits – at least two years in the UK. Service credited through a transfer from a previous employer's scheme counts towards qualifying service.

Rebate-only personal pension: an APP which is funded entirely from contracted-out rebates paid to the provider by the Department for Social Security.

Reduction in premium: see **Charge ratio**.

Reduction in yield: the difference between the gross return to a pension fund and the return earned net of charges.

Regulation: the setting of rules – regulations – which govern the behaviour of participants in a market so as to achieve a set of desired outcomes. Regulations may be negative or positive. Negative regulations prohibit undesirable activities, e.g. rules to prevent pension fund managers from taking excessive risks with members' funds. Positive regulations promote desirable activities, e.g. rules to ensure that pension schemes maintain an adequate balance between assets and liabilities. Since regulation can give rise to compliance costs for those whose actions are regulated, regulators must try to balance the cost and desirability of achieving a particular outcome. Problems associated with Britain's MFR and FRS 17 are, arguably, examples of how regulation can sometimes be counterproductive.

Replacement rate (income replacement rate): the level of income provided by a pension at retirement expressed as a proportion of pre-retirement earnings. In the UK, DB occupational schemes typically aim to provide a level of income replacement at retirement equal to two-thirds or one-half of pre-retirement earnings after 40 years of contributions. By contrast, the replacement rate provided by the BSP is around 15 per cent of average male earnings. See also **Effective replacement rate**.

Retirement age (pension age): the age at which individuals become eligible to receive a retirement pension, not necessarily the age at which they actually retire. See also **Effective retirement age**.

Retirement annuity: see **Section 226 plans**.

Retirement benefits: cash or other benefits received by retired people. Although the term usually refers to payments from a pension scheme, it is sometimes used in reference to goods or services that retirees can receive free of charge, or at a discount, that working people must pay for in full.

Retirement income system: see **Pension system**.

Sandler Report: a report on Britain's medium and long-term savings industry by Ron Sandler, a former chief executive of Lloyd's of London, published on 9 July 2002. The Report contained the findings of a review carried out by Sandler – commissioned by the Treasury on 18 June 2001 –

aimed at finding ways to raise the level of medium and long-term saving in Britain. Sandler identified several factors which discouraged saving, especially amongst low- to middle-income groups. These included high charges, due to weak competition and high fixed costs of advice, and complex products which were difficult to compare and offered poor value for money. He recommended that a range of simplified savings products be introduced, which could be bought without the need for expensive advice. These products would be modelled on the new stakeholder pensions, having no up-front commissions, with charges limited to 1 per cent of savers' funds.

Savings gap: the difference between what people need to save each year in order to obtain an adequate retirement income – usually taken to be two-thirds of their pre-retirement earnings – and the amount they actually save. Its calculation depends upon assumptions about the magnitude of variables such as annuity rates and the rate of return to saving. The lower annuity rates and the rate of return to saving are assumed to be, the greater will be the savings gap. According to estimates produced for the ABI, in 2001 the UK's savings gap totalled £27 billion, based on an assumed annual rate of return of 7 per cent.

Scheme deficit: see **Under-funded scheme**.

Scheme-specific funding standards: a way of measuring the solvency of funded DB occupational pension schemes which takes account of their individual circumstances rather than forcing them to comply with a common asset–liability ratio. Thus, a scheme with a relatively low asset–liability ratio may be deemed to be solvent if its liabilities are mostly long term and its investment strategy is geared towards growth. Conversely, a scheme with a higher asset–liability ratio may be deemed insolvent if it is invested in assets the market prices of which are volatile and its liabilities are mostly short term. In 2001, the government announced that the MFR was to be scrapped and replaced with scheme-specific funding standards as recommended in the Myners Report.

Scheme surplus: see **Over-funded scheme**.

Section 226 plans: forerunners of approved personal pension plans. These were DC plans provided by insurance companies and friendly societies, which were available to the self-employed and to employees who wanted to opt out of the state earnings-related pension scheme, but whose employers did not provide a DB scheme.

Self-administered scheme (directly invested scheme): an occupational pension scheme the assets of which are invested directly by its trustees or on their behalf by an in-house or an external investment manager. The majority of large DB occupational schemes in the UK are of the self-administered type.

Self-Invested Personal Pension (SIPP): a UK personal pension plan where plan-holders are able to choose the assets in which their fund is invested. Permissible investments include equities and bonds, unit trusts and property. SIPPs, contributions to which attract the same tax relief as those to conventional PPPs, have become more popular recently, due in part to a loss of confidence in the professionally managed products offered by insurance companies.

Self-investment: investment by an occupational pension fund in the equities of its sponsoring employer. To protect contributors from the risks associated with over-investment in the shares of a single company, governments often place limits on the proportions of occupational funds that may be self-invested. For example, UK occupational schemes may not normally invest more than 5 per cent of their funds in the equities of their sponsoring firms. The dangers of excessive self-investment were brought into focus with the collapse of the US energy firm Enron. With around 60 per cent of Enron's 401(K) fund invested in the company's own shares, contributors' retirement savings were all but wiped out when the firm went bust in December 2001.

Seniority pension: an arrangement whereby workers become eligible for a pension after so many years of service, even if they have not reached the official retirement age.

Service Credits: see also: **Added years**.

Shortfall risk: the possibility that sponsors may have to make emergency payments into their funded DB schemes if the value of assets falls below liabilities. Shortfall risk will be significant where schemes invest heavily in volatile assets like equities and where there are strict solvency rules. See also **Deficiency payments**.

Social insurance scheme: a public pension scheme which seeks to provide a post-retirement standard of living similar to that enjoyed during a person's working life through the provision of earnings-related benefits financed from earnings-related contributions. Social insurance schemes are more expensive to provide than basic income schemes, because the benefits they provide are higher.

Social security: the term used to denote the public pension scheme in America. In the UK, it is an arrangement for delivering a variety of publicly-provided welfare benefits such as pensions, sickness and disability benefits and unemployment pay, financed from compulsory social security contributions. Entitlement to receive social security benefits is determined with reference to a person's contributions record and sometimes a means test.

Solvency: the ability of a funded DB scheme to pay its members the retirement benefits to which they are entitled. A scheme that would be insolvent if it were wound up immediately may be solvent on an ongoing basis, if its assets are growing faster than its liabilities. Since the rate at which liabilities will grow and the level of future contributions and investment returns cannot be known with certainty, whether or not a scheme is judged to be solvent on an ongoing basis depends upon the assumptions actuaries make about these variables.

Stakeholder pension: a low-cost and flexible individual pension plan introduced in the UK in 2001, which is designed to be attractive to individuals with low to middle incomes. Annual charges are capped at 1 per cent of the value of contributors' funds, and contributions, which may be stopped and started at will, can be as low as £20. At least three-quarters of individuals' terminal funds must be annuitised between the ages of 50 and 75, and up to 25 per cent may be taken as a tax-free lump sum. Employers with five or more employees are required by law to provide their workers with access to a stakeholder pension, although they cannot compel them to join and do not have to make contributions on their behalf. See also **Personal pension plan**.

Statement of Investment Principles (SIP): a document prepared by occupational pension scheme trustees setting out the current investment aims of their funds. Like the scheme's trust deeds, SIPs may contain limits on the investment options available to fund managers. They may, for example, prohibit investment in certain types of asset, e.g. private equities.

State pension Scheme: see **Public Pension Scheme**.

State Second Pension (S2P): the British state supplementary pension scheme which began to be phased in in place of SERPS in April 2003. Membership of S2P, which will provide superior benefits to SERPS, will eventually be restricted to workers with modest incomes. Although contributions to S2P will initially earn entitlement to earnings-related benefits with a higher replacement rate than SERPS, in the long run the new scheme will provide low earners with a flat-rate top-up to the BSP.

Statutory Money Purchase Illustration (SMPI): an illustration which money purchase pension providers have, since April 2003, been legally required to provide, showing how much an individual's pension is projected to be worth at retirement in current prices. SMPIs currently assume a 7 per cent annual rate of return on investments, 2.5 per cent inflation, and that individuals work until age 65. They also assume that terminal funds are used to purchase an indexed joint-life annuity. Although DC pension providers were obliged to give plan-holders annual forecasts before SMPIs were introduced, these often showed projected terminal fund values rather than illustrations of actual retirement incomes.

Superannuation: another name for a pension scheme.

Superannuation Guarantee Charge (SGC): a requirement, introduced in 1992, for Australian employers to make contributions to DC pension plans on behalf of their employees. The introduction of the SGC raised occupational pension coverage from around 50 per cent in the late 1980s to nearly 100 per cent today. The contribution rate for employers is currently 9 per cent of employees' earnings, although some would like to see this rise to 12 per cent. Around half of all Australian workers also make voluntary contributions.

Supervision: ensuring that individuals and organisations who are subject to regulation are in compliance with the rules governing their behaviour. Supervisors monitor the actions of regulated individuals and organisations and may apply sanctions where rules are breached. In Britain, responsibility for the supervision of private pension providers lies mainly with OPRA and the FSA.

Supplementary pension: a pension which supplements the retirement income provided by a first-tier state scheme. Supplementary pensions may be provided by the state, employers and commercial pension providers. National differences in the proportion of total pension income that derives from supplementary pensions is largely a reflection of differences in the generosity of first-tier state schemes. Increasing the share of total pension incomes that comes from supplementary pensions – especially supplementary private pensions – is a key element in pension reforms around the world.

Support ratio: the ratio of workers to pensioners in a pay-as-you-go pension scheme. Declining support ratios are an inevitable consequence of population ageing. Other things being equal, a fall in the support ratio will mean that contributions must rise or benefits fall if a scheme is to remain in financial equilibrium.

Survivors' benefits: see **Death benefits**.

Take-up (Participation): the proportion of individuals who are eligible to participate in some arrangement, e.g. a pension scheme, who actually do so. Ignorance and inertia, as well as means tests in the case of welfare benefits, are frequent reasons why take-up is less than 100 per cent.

Targeted money purchase scheme: a money purchase scheme which aims to provide a specified level of retirement income, but does not promise to do so.

Targeting: focusing tax-financed welfare benefits on those who need them most. Targeting is one way governments attempt to keep down the cost of providing retirees with non-pension benefits such as help with housing costs and income support. See also **Means-test**.

Tax expenditure: the value of taxes forgone where income contributed to pension schemes – and/or the investment returns earned on contributions

– is exempt from taxation or taxed at a lower rate than other income. To limit the scale of tax expenditures, governments often place restrictions on the amount of income that may be contributed to a pension scheme in a single year.

Temporary annuity: an annuity providing an income stream for a limited period. Temporary annuities may or may not terminate with the death of the annuitant. See also **Guaranteed annuity**.

Terminal fund: the money in a DC pension plan at the end of the accumulation phase.

Tontines: annuity pools set up by groups of investors in seventeenth century France. Members of a *tontine* received a life annuity in return for a single up-front payment. When a member died, his or her annuity payments were shared out among the surviving members. Thus, the value of annuities from a *tontine* increased over time. When there was only one member still living, he or she collected the remaining fund, and the *tontine* was terminated.

Top hat scheme: an individually-insured pension plan, where participation is restricted to particular company executives and/or key workers.

Total dependency ratio: see **Youth dependency ratio**.

Total earnings scheme: a form of career average scheme where the value of pension entitlements is calculated as a fixed proportion of an employee's aggregate earnings during his or her period of membership.

Transferability: the term used to denote the extent to which pension rights accrued in a DB plan can be transferred to another scheme, whether of the DB or DC type. See also **Portability**.

Transfer circuit (transfer club): an arrangement between a group of employers for transfers between their pension schemes to be made using a standardised method of calculating transfer values. The use of a common method of valuing liabilities means that workers who move between employers in a transfer circuit are not subject to the portability losses that can otherwise arise. In the UK, a transfer circuit exists between public sector schemes.

Transfer ratio: the annual share of a country's national income going to public pension payments divided by the proportion of pensioners to people of working age, i.e. the pensions burden divided by the old-age dependency ratio. The calculation of transfer ratios allows international comparisons of public pension costs to be made that take account of differences in the relative size of pensioner populations.

Transfer value: the cash equivalent of an individual's accrued benefit entitlements in a DB pension scheme which may be transferred into an alternative scheme. The alternative scheme may also be of the DB type, or it might be a DC plan. Transfer values are calculated as the cost of providing early leavers with their accrued pension entitlements at prevailing annuity rates. Consequently, timing is an important determinant of transfer values, since these will be higher when annuity rates are low than when they are high.

Trust: a legal arrangement whereby assets are held by trustees on behalf of others – the beneficiaries. The terms on which individuals may become beneficiaries and the benefits to which they will be entitled are set out in the trust deed. In Britain, occupational pension schemes are usually established as trusts and must be run in accordance with UK trust law.

Trustee: an individual or a company who has been appointed to carry out the purposes of a trust as set out in the trust deed. Trustees, who may also be beneficiaries, must discharge their duties in accordance with UK trust law. Failure to do so can result in trustees being dismissed, fined or even imprisoned. In Britain, the majority of trustees of occupational pension schemes are appointed by the sponsoring employer. This situation has led some people to question their independence.

Under-funded scheme (scheme deficit): a situation where, as a result of an actuarial valuation, a funded DB pension scheme is found to hold assets of insufficient value to cover all its liabilities. A scheme may become under-funded due to a fall in the market value of the assets it holds or the returns they yield, an unanticipated increase in its liabilities, or because contributions are inadequate. In Britain, responsibility for making good a scheme deficit lies with the sponsor, who is given a limited period in which to do this. Deficits may be reduced through a benefit reduction (where the rules of the scheme permit), an increase in employer contributions or a cash payment into the scheme by the sponsor. See also **Deficiency payment**.

Unit-linked annuity: an annuity contract which provides an income based on the price of units in a unitised investment fund run by the insurance company that sold it. These contracts are similar to with-profits annuities, but the income they provide can be much more variable because it is not subject to smoothing. Because the income provided by a unit-linked annuity is linked to stockmarket returns it has the potential to rise substantially. It can also fall substantially. Thus, unit-linked annuities are unsuitable for individuals who need a stable income in retirement. See also **With-profits annuity**.

Unit trust: a trust established as a pooled investment fund with a portfolio of investments which is divided into discrete units. Investors may buy into a unit trust, or liquidate an existing investment, through the purchase or sale of units, the prices of which are set by the fund managers. Life assurance policies, mortgage endowment plans and pensions are frequently linked to unit trusts.

Universal basic pension: a minimum pension benefit payable to everyone who reaches pensionable age. Pure universal basic pension schemes are non-contributory. They aim to prevent poverty in old age through the provision of flat-rate benefits which are financed out of general taxation. Although Britain's basic state pension is virtually universal, it provides flat-rate benefits which are funded from earnings-related contributions.

Upper Earnings Limit (UEL): a limit on the amount of earnings on which full UK National Insurance contributions are payable. The UEL was set at £30,420 (£585 per week) for the 2002–2003 fiscal year. Full National Insurance contributions are not payable on earnings above this level. Since 6 April 2003, however, National Insurance contributions of 1 per cent are payable on all earnings above the UEL. See also **Lower earnings limit**.

Uprating: see **Indexation**.

Vested rights: the accrued benefit entitlements of the members of a DB scheme, which constitute its pension liabilities. These include pensions in payment, the deferred pensions of individuals who have left the scheme, the accrued entitlements of current contributors and, where applicable, the benefit rights of past and present members' survivors and dependants.

Vesting period: the interval between an employee joining an occupational pension scheme and actually becoming entitled to receive retirement benefits. Vesting periods are a means by which employers can promote staff loyalty, since employees who leave during the vesting period forfeit their accrued retirement benefits. Lengthy vesting periods are particularly problematic for women, who tend to change jobs more frequently than men, and typically have shorter average job tenure. For the economy as a whole, long vesting periods may undermine economic performance by reducing the flexibility of the labour market. A solution to both these problems is to have shorter vesting periods.

Voluntary annuity: see **Purchased life annuity**.

Waiting period: a period of service which must be served by employees before they become entitled to join an occupational pension scheme. By making the right to join the company scheme a reward for loyal service, waiting periods can facilitate staff retention. Some schemes treat the waiting periods served by employees who become members as pensionable service. Even so, waiting periods can be problematic for workers who change jobs frequently and are thus prevented from accruing any occupational pension rights. See also **Qualifying service, Vesting period**.

Winding up: the process of terminating an occupational pension scheme. When a DB scheme is wound up, its assets and liabilities may be transferred to another scheme. Alternatively, members' pension rights may be protected through the purchase of immediate and deferred annuities.

Problems can arise when an under-funded scheme is wound up, because there may be insufficient assets available to cover the benefit entitlements of all members. In the case of well-funded schemes, however, winding up can be a means of liberating excess funds which sponsors may seek to capture for their own benefit.

With-profits annuity: an annuity contract the performance of which is linked to the bonuses paid out from a with-profits fund run by the insurance company that sold it. Although the income provided by with-profits annuities is initially lower than could be obtained from some other types of annuity, it has the potential to rise to a much higher level. A possible drawback of with-profits annuities, however, is that increases in annual payments are less certain than they are with an indexed or an escalating annuity. See also **With-profits fund**.

With-profits fund: a fund run by an insurance company which is invested predominantly in equities, but also includes bonds, property and other non-equity investments. The investment returns earned by with-profits funds are paid to investors in the form of annual bonuses which may or may not be reinvested. To iron out stockmarket fluctuations, some of the returns earned in 'good' years are reserved, being added to bonuses in 'bad' years. Thus annual bonuses are smoothed over time so as to provide more stable returns to investors. In addition, many funds offer investors a guaranteed minimum rate of return. Life assurance policies, mortgage endowment plans and pension annuities are frequently linked to with-profits funds.

Workforce (labour force): the population group comprising all individuals of working age, i.e. those who have left school but have not yet reached state pension age. The workforce is not a measure of the numbers actually in employment, since some people of working age will be unemployed or unable to work due to sickness or disability. Others will have no need to work, or may be kept from paid employment by the need to care for children or other dependent relatives. Thus, the workforce is a measure of a country's potential, rather than its actual, supply of labour. See also **Labour market participation rate**.

Youth dependency ratio: the ratio of young people in a population to those of working age. It is most commonly calculated as the ratio of people aged 0–15 years to those aged between 16 and state pension age. The youth dependency ratio is important because, even more than the old, young people are economically dependent upon the working population. The youth dependency ratio can be summed with the old-age dependency ratio to give the total dependency ratio. Because today's low rates of fertility are expected to persist, the youth dependency ratio is projected to fall during the coming decades. Consequently, the decline in the youth dependency ratio will, to some extent, offset the effect of forecast increases in the old-age dependency ratio on the total dependency ratio.

References

Aaron, H. J. (1966) 'The Social Insurance Paradox', *Canadian Journal Of Economics*, 32, 371–7.

ACA (2002) *Occupational Pensions: The Widening Gap*, Association of Consulting Actuaries.

Attanasio, O. P., Emmerson, C. (2001) *Differential Mortality in the UK*, Working Paper No 01/16, Institute for Fiscal Studies.

Auerbach, A., Gokhale, J., Kotlikoff, L. J. (1994) 'Generational accounting: a meaningful way to evaluate fiscal policy', *Journal of Economic Perspectives*, 8(1), 73–94.

Baker, D., Weisbrot, M. (1999) *Social Security. The Phony Crisis*, University of Chicago Press.

Banks, J., Emmerson, C. (2000) 'Public and private pension spending: principles, practice and the need for reform', *Fiscal Studies*, 21(1), 1–63.

Banks, J., Blundell, R., Disney, R., Emmerson, C. (2002) *Retirement Pensions and the Adequacy of Saving: A Guide to the Debate*, Briefing Note No. 29, Institute for Fiscal Studies, October.

Barham, C. (2003) 'Life stages of economic inactivity', *Labour Market Trends*, 111(10), 495–502.

Beveridge, W. (1942) *Social Insurance and Allied Services*, HMSO.

Blake, D. (1992) *Issues in Pension Funding*, Routledge.

Blake, D. (2000) 'Does it matter what pension scheme you have?' *Economic Journal*, February, 45–81.

Blundell, S., Scarpetta, S. (1998) *Falling Participation Rates Among Older Workers in the OECD Countries: The Role of Social Security Systems*, Organisation for Economic Cooperation and Development.

Blundell, R., Tanner, S. (1999) *Labour Force Participation and Retirement in the UK*, Institute for Fiscal Studies. Available at http://www.ifs.org.uk/pensions/olderworkers.pdf.

Boldrin, M., Dolado, J., Jimeno, J., Peracchi, F. (1999) 'The future of pensions in Europe', *Economic Policy*, October, 289–320.

Booth, P., Cooper, D. (2002) 'The tax treatment of UK defined contribution pension schemes', *Fiscal Studies*, 23(1), 77–104.

Brugiavini, A., Fornero, E. (2001) 'Pension provision in Italy', in Disney, R., Johnson, P. (eds) *Pension Systems and Retirement Incomes Across OECD Countries*, Edward Elgar Publishing Ltd, 197–235.

Cardarelli, R., Sefton, J., Kotlikoff, L. J. (1999) *Generational Accounting in the UK*, National Institute for Economic and Social Research.

Carter, M., Shipman, W. (1996) *Promises to Keep: Saving Social Security's Dream,* Regnery Publishing.

Chia, N., Tsui, A. (2003) 'Life annuities of compulsory savings and income adequacy of the elderly in Singapore', *Journal of Pension Economics and FInance,* 2(1), 41–65.

Clark, T., Emmerson, C. (2003) 'Privatising provision and attacking poverty? The direction of UK pension policy under New Labour', *Journal of Pension Economics and Finance,* 2(1), 67–89.

Council of Europe. (1998) *Recent Demographic Developments in Europe,* Strasbourg.

Curry, C. (2001) 'To Save or not to Save: The Impact of the Pension Credit', *Insurance Trends,* January, pp. 7–16.

Davis, E. P. (1995) *Pension Funds: Retirement-Income Security, and Capital Markets,* Clarendon Press.

Davis, E. P. (2001) *The Regulation of Funded Pensions – A Case Study of the United Kingdom,* Occasional Paper Series No. 15, Financial Services Authority.

DHSS (1985), *Reform of Social Security,* Department of Health and Social Security, CMMD 9517, HMSO.

Diamond, P. (2002) *Social Security Reform,* Oxford University Press.

Dilnot, A., Johnson, P. (1993) *The Taxation of Private Pensions,* Institute for Fiscal Studies.

Dilnot, A., Disney, R., Johnson, P., Whitehouse, E. (1994) *Pensions Policy in the UK: An Economic Analysis,* Institute for Fiscal Studies, London.

Disney, R., Johnson, P. (eds) (2001) *Pension Systems and Retirement Incomes Across OECD Countries,* Edward Elgar.

Disney, R., Whitehouse, E. (1992) *The Personal Pensions Stampede,* Institute for Fiscal Studies, London.

Disney, R., Whitehouse, E. (2001) *Cross-Country Comparisons of Pensioners' Incomes,* DSS Research Report No. 142, Department for Social Security, Leeds.

DSS (1998) *A New Contract for Welfare: A Partnership in Pensions,* Department for Social Security, Leeds.

Dunnell, K. (2000) *Policy Responses to Population Ageing and Population Decline,* United Kingdom Office for National Statistics.

DWP (2002) *Simplicity, Security and Choice: Working and Saving for Retirement,* Department for Work and Pensions, December.

DWP (2003) *The Pensioners' Incomes Series 2001/2,* First Release, Department for Work and Pensions, June.

Emmerson, C., Johnson, P. (2003) 'Pension Provision in the United Kingdom', in Disney, R., Johnson, P. (eds) *Pension Systems and Retirement Incomes Across OECD Countries,* Edward Elgar Publishing Limited, pp. 296–333.

Engen, E., Gale, W., Scholz, J. (1996) 'The illusory effects of saving incentives on saving', *Journal of Economic Perspectives,* 10(4), 113–138.

Falkingham, J., Johnson, P. (1993) *A Unified Funded Pension Scheme (UFPS) for Britain,* Welfare State Programme (WSP) Discussion Paper No 90, London School of Economics, April.

Falkingham, J., Rake, K. (2001) *British Pension Reform and the Pension Credit: A Response to the Pension Credit Consultation Document,* SAGE Discussion Paper No. 6, February.

Feldstein, M. (1996) 'The missing piece in policy analysis: social security reform', *American Economic Review, Papers and Proceedings,* 86, 1–14.

Forni, L., Giordano, R. (2001) 'Funding a PAYG Pension System: the Case of Italy', *Fiscal Studies*, 22(4), 487–526.

Friedman, B., Warshawsky, M. (1990) 'The Cost of Annuities: Implications for Savings Behaviour and Bequests', *Quarterly Journal of Economics*, 105, 135–54.

Fries, J. F. (1980) 'Ageing, Natural Death and the Compression of Morbidity', *New England Journal of Medicine*, 303, 130–136.

Fries, J. F. (1988) 'Ageing, Illness and Health Policy Implications of the Compression of Morbidity', *Perspectives in Biology and Medicine*, 31(3), 407–423.

Fries, J. F. (1989) 'The Compression of Morbidity: Near or Far', *The Milbank Memorial Fund Quarterly*, 67(2), 208–232.

Financial Times (2002) 'Why living too long is bad for our pensions: The Pickering Report', *Financial Times*, 13 July, p. 4

GAD (2003) *Occupational Pension Schemes 2000 – Eleventh Survey by the Government Actuary – Preliminary Results for Public Sector Schemes*, Government Actuary's Department.

Goodman, A., Myck. M., Shephard, A. (2003) *Sharing in the Nation's Prosperity? Pensioner Poverty in Britain*, Institution for Fiscal Studies, Commentary, P. 93.

Grainge, E., Segars, J., Curry, C. (2002) 'One Year on – Stakeholders Revealed', *Insurance Trends*, April, pp. 1–12.

Griffiths, I. (1986) *Creative Accounting*, Firethorn.

Hall, M. (1991) 'The Savings and Loans Debacle: A Regulatory Nightmare', *National Westminster Bank Quarterly Review*, November, pp 2–13.

Herbertsson, T., Orszag, J., Orszag, P. (2000) *The Nordic Pension Systems*, Discussion Papers in Economics, 6/2000, Department of Economics, Birkbeck College, University of London.

Hinde, A. (1998) *Demographic Methods*, Arnold.

Howells, P., Bain, K. (1998) *The Economics of Money, Banking and Finance*, Longman.

Inland Revenue (2002) *Simplifying the Taxation of Pensions, Increasing Choice and Flexibility for All*, Inland Revenue, December.

Jackson, S. (1998) *Britain's Population*, Routledge.

Johnson, P. (1992), *Income: Pensions, Earnings and Savings in the Third Age*, The Carnegie United Kingdom Trust.

Keenay, G., Whitehouse, E. (2003) 'The Role of the Personal Tax System in Old-Age Support: A Survey of 15 Countries', *Fiscal Studies*, 24(1), 1–21.

King, A., Baekgaard, H., Harding, A. (2001) 'Pension Provision in Australia', in Disney, R., Johnson, P. (eds) *Pension Systems and Retirement Incomes Across OECD Countries*, Edward Elgar, Publishing Ltd, 48–91.

Kotlikoff, L. J. (1992) *Generational Accounting: Knowing Who Pays, and When, for What We Spend*, The Free Press.

Miles, D. (1998) 'The Implications of Switching from Unfunded to Funded Pension Systems', *National Institute Economic Review*, 163, 71–86.

Mittelstaedt, H. F. (2003) 'An Empirical Analysis of the Investment Performance of the Chilean Pension System', *Journal of Pension Economics and Finance*, 2, 7–24.

Mullan, P. (2000) *The Imaginary Time Bomb*, I. B. Tauris.

Murthi, M., Orszag, J. M., Orszag, P. (1999) *The Value for Money of Annuities in the UK: Theory, Experience and Policy*, Discussion Papers in Economics, 19/99, Birkbeck College, University of London.

Occupational Pensions Board (1997) *Occupational Pensions Board Final Report: 1973-1997*, Occupational Pensions Board, London.

Office for National Statistics (2002) 'Social Protection,' *Social Trends*, 32, 147.

Orszag, J. M. (2000) *Annuities: the Problems,* Discussion Papers in Economics, 7/2000, Department of Economics, Birkbeck College, University of London.

OWC (2001) *The Future Regulation of UK Savings and Investment: Targeting the Savings Gap*, Oliver Wyman and Co. Available at http://www.abi.org.uk/oliver-wymanreport.pdf.

Peterson, P. G. (1999) 'Gray Dawn: The Global Aging Crisis' *Foreign Affairs*, January/February, pp. 42–55.

Pickering, A. (2002) *A Simpler Way to Better Pensions: An Independent Report by Alan Pickering*, Department for Work and Pensions, London.

Poterba, J. (2001) 'Annuity Markets and Retirement Security', *Fiscal Studies*, 22(3), 249–70.

Samuelson, P. A. (1958) An Exact Consumption-Loan Model of Interest With or Without the Social Contrivance of Money, *Journal of Political Economy*, 66, 467–82.

Sandler, R. (2002) *Medium and Long Term Retail Savings in the UK: A Review*, HM Treasury.

Sass, S. (1997) *The Promise of Private Pensions*, Harvard University Press.

Segars, J. (2002) 'Closing the Savings Gap – Carrots or Sticks?', *Insurance Trends*, July, pp. 10–20.

Smeaton, D., McKay, S. (2003) *Working after State Pension Age: Quantitative Analysis,* DWP Research Report Series, No. 182.

Stark, J., Curry, C. (2001) 'Is There an "Annuity Problem?"', *Insurance Trends,* April, pp. 1–11.

Stark, J., Curry, C. (2002) 'Reforming Annuities: Big Bang or Softly, Softly?', *Insurance Trends,* January, pp. 1–14.

Stears, G. (2003) 'Research Update: How Much in Funded Pensions in 2001?', *Insurance Trends Quarterly Statistics Research Review*, 38, 40–42.

Sullivan, M. (1996a) 'Privatizing Pensions: a Response to the Crisis in Public Policy' in Braddon D. Foster D.(eds) *Privatization: Social Science Themes and Perspectives*, Dartmouth, pp. 159–182.

Sullivan, M. (1996b) 'The Part-time Phenomenon', in Victoria de Elizagarate, *Revista De Direccion Y Administracion De Empresas*, 5, 103–18.

Thane, P. (ed.) (1978) *The Origins of British Social Policy,* Croom Helm, London.

Thane, P. (2000) *Old Age in English History,* Oxford University Press.

Turner, J. (1998) Retirement Income Systems for Different Economic, Demographic and Political Environments, Working Paper AWP3, 8, OECD.

Victor, C. (1991) 'Continuity or change: inequalities in health in later life', *Ageing and Society*, 11, 23–29.

Wallace, P. (2001) *Agequake,* Nicholas Brealey Publishing.

Weller, C. (2000) *Raising the Retirement Age. The Wrong Direction for Social Security,* Economic Policy Institute, Briefing Paper, Washington DC, September.

Wilson, T. (1974) *Pensions, Inflation and Growth*, Heinemann.

World Bank (1994) *Averting the Old-Age Crisis,* Oxford University Press.

Index

Page numbers in *italic* refer to tables and figures.

eBooks – at www.eBookstore.tandf.co.uk

A library at your fingertips!

eBooks are electronic versions of printed books. You can store them on your PC/laptop or browse them online.

They have advantages for anyone needing rapid access to a wide variety of published, copyright information.

eBooks can help your research by enabling you to bookmark chapters, annotate text and use instant searches to find specific words or phrases. Several eBook files would fit on even a small laptop or PDA.

NEW: Save money by eSubscribing: cheap, online access to any eBook for as long as you need it.

Annual subscription packages

We now offer special low-cost bulk subscriptions to packages of eBooks in certain subject areas. These are available to libraries or to individuals.

For more information please contact webmaster.ebooks@tandf.co.uk

We're continually developing the eBook concept, so keep up to date by visiting the website.

www.eBookstore.tandf.co.uk